A MOUTHFUL OF BIRDS
BY CARYL CHURCHILL AND DAVID LAN

A Methuen New Theatrescript
published by Methuen
in association with Joint Stock Theatre Group

METHUEN'S NEW THEATRESCRIPTS

First published as a paperback original in 1986 by Methuen London Ltd,
11 New Fetter Lane, London EC4P 4EE in association with Joint Stock Theatre Group,
123 Tottenham Court Road, London W1P 9HN.

Copyright © 1986 by Caryl Churchill and David Lan
Photographs reproduced by courtesy of Phil Cutts

British Library Cataloguing in Publication Data

Churchill, Caryl
    A mouthful of birds: a text written
    for the Joint Stock Theatre Group.———
    (A Methuen new theatrescript)
    I. Title   II. Lan, David   III. Joint Stock
    Theatre Group   IV. Euripides. Bacchae
    822'.914   PR6053.H786

    ISBN 0-413-15460-2

Cover artwork by Central Station Design
Printed in Great Britain by Expression Printers Ltd, London N7

CAUTION
This play is fully protected by copyright. All rights reserved and all enquiries concerning the rights for professional or amateur stage productions should be made to Margaret Ramsay Ltd, 14a Goodwin's Court, St Martin's Lane, London WC2N 4LL. A video showing the choreography by Ian Spink is obtainable from Harriet Cruickshank, 97 Old South Lambeth Road, London SW8 1XU.

JOINT STOCK THEATRE GROUP
AND
BIRMINGHAM REPERTORY THEATRE
present

A MOUTHFUL OF BIRDS

by CARYL CHURCHILL and DAVID LAN

LENA, *a Mother*	Tricia Kelly
MARCIA, *a Switchboard Operator*	Dona Croll
DEREK, *Unemployed*	Christian Burgess
YVONNE, *an Acupuncturist*	Vivienne Rochester
PAUL, *a Businessman*	Philippe Girandeau
DAN, *a Vicar*	Stephen Goff
DOREEN, *a Secretary*	Amelda Brown
DIONYSOS	Philippe Giraudeau
PENTHEUS, *King of Thebes*	Christian Burgess
AGAVE, *his Mother*	Amelda Brown
WOMEN	Dona Croll, Tricia Kelly, Vivienne Rochester
DIONYSOS 2	Stephen Goff

Other parts are played by members of the company

Psychic Attack

Lena	Tricia Kelly
Roy	Christian Burgess
Spirit	Stephen Goff

Baron Sunday

Marcia	Dona Croll
Decima	Vivienne Rochester
Sybil	Amelda Brown
Margaret	Tricia Kelly
Musicologist	Philippe Giraudeau

Dancing

Dan	Stephen Goff
Prison Officers	Christian Burgess
	Amelda Brown
Victims	Dona Croll
	Philippe Giraudeau
	Vivienne Rochester

Pig

Paul	Philippe Giraudeau
Pig	Stephen Goff

Colleagues	Vivienne Rochester
	Amelda Brown
Friend	Christian Burgess
June	Dona Croll
Wrapper	Tricia Kelly

Interval of fifteen minutes

Herculine Barbin

Derek	Christian Burgess
Herculine	Tricia Kelly

Gold Shoes

Yvonne	Vivienne Rochester
Mother	Dona Croll
Women	Tricia Kelly
	Amelda Brown

Hot Summer

Doreen	Amelda Brown
Mrs Blair	Dona Croll
Suzy	Vivienne Rochester
Lil	Tricia Kelly
Tony	Stephen Goff
Mr Evans	Philippe Giraudeau

Written by	Caryl Churchill and David Lan
Directed by	Ian Spink and Les Waters
Designed by	Annie Smart
Lighting designed by	Rick Fisher
Production and Company Manager	Alan Day
Stage Managers	Christine Hathway, Hilary Russell
Lighting Technician	Nick Kirkpatrick
Poster Design	Central Station Design, Manchester
Photographs	Phil Cutts
Voice Coach	Bardie Thomas

For Joint Stock

Administrator	Jane Dawson
Press and publicity	Di Speirs

On Saturday 11th October Amelda Brown took over the roles initially played by Marjorie Yates. Marjorie Yates was a member of the original workshop company and cast.

After its three week run at Birmingham Repertory Theatre, *A Mouthful of Birds* tours throughout the autumn. The production plays at the following theatres: Stahl Theatre, Oundle (23-24 September), Stanwix Theatre, Carlisle (25-27 September), Theatre Royal and Opera House, Wakefield (29 September-4 October), Theatre Royal, Winchester (8-11 October), The Everyman, Cheltenham (13-14 October), Essex University (16-18 October), Warwick Arts Centre (21-25 October), Sherman Theatre, Cardiff (27 October-1 November), Nuffield Studio, Lancaster (4-8 November), Arts Theatre, Cambridge (10-15 November), The Gardner Centre, Brighton (18-22 November) and The Royal Court Theatre, London (26 November-20 December).

Credits
Costume, Scenery, Properties and Wigs made in the Theatre Production Department at Birmingham Repertory Theatre. Wardrobe care by Persil Automatic, Lux and Comfort, courtesy of Lever Brothers. Fabric Finish and Robin Spray Starch from Reckitt Products. Dry Cleaning by Mini Cleaners. The Rep is cleaned by We are Cleaning (Birmingham) Ltd.
We gratefully acknowledge the assistance of the following companies with this production: Clingfilm by GELPACK (Snappies) Limited and the telephone by Tandy's (Birmingham).
The Birmingham Repertory Theatre receives financial assistance from the Arts Council of Great Britain and the City of Birmingham.
Joint Stock receives financial assistance from the Arts Council of Great Britain.

AUTHORS' NOTES

The Workshop and the Play

We started with an interest in possession and in women being violent – two things that come together in *The Bacchae*, which is why we took it as one of the starting points for the workshop.

I had been thinking before the workshop about women and violence. Women have traditionally been seen as more peaceful than men, and that view has been politicised, particularly by women protesting against nuclear weapons. There is a danger of polarising men and women into what becomes again the traditional view that men are naturally more violent and so have no reason to change. It seems important to recognise women's capacity for violence and men's for peacefulness. There is a difference between women able to be peaceable because they wave men off to war and women who recognise their own capacity for violence but choose not to use it. *The Bacchae* is about a violent murder done by women; it is about the pleasure of physical power, the exhilaration of destruction, and finally a recognition of its horror. We became interested too in the way the authoritarian Pentheus, trying to maintain state power by official armed violence, is subverted by the androgynous god.

We didn't intend to do a version of *The Bacchae* but to look at the same issues of possession, violence and ecstasy. 'I don't know what got into me' is a common experience for us all in some form, and we looked at our own moments of being beside ourselves. We went to mediums who gave us messages from our dead relatives; we listened to experiences of a woman given instructions by spirits, women who have been violent, a transsexual who is now a woman, and many others. Some of us were hypnotised and taken back to previous lives, some had a night out with two hundred women watching drag acts and male strippers, most of us spent a couple of days living and sleeping in the open. Days and nights without our usual routines seemed long and full of possibilities – from this came the idea of an 'undefended day' in which there is nothing to protect you from the forces inside and outside yourself. This led to the play finally taking the form of seven people stopping their usual lives and having 'undefended days', the main scenes of the play, in which each person is possessed, by a spirit or a passion. At the end of *The Bacchae*, Agave gives up following Dionysos, but in this play she and the other women stay on the mountain, accepting that they can't go back to their previous lives and welcoming further change; and all the characters change again in their final speeches into new lives that develop from what happened to them while they were possessed.

We could have left the play as the seven stories without including anything from *The Bacchae* itself, but would have missed the presence of that horrific murder and possession, something not invented by us or by Euripides, so we kept it as something that bursts from the past into these people open to possession, first the voice of an unquiet spirit telling of a murder, finally the murder itself happening as the climax to all their stories.

CARYL CHURCHILL
Autumn, 1986

The Politics of Ecstasy

We began with *The Bacchae* and the idea of possession.

Almost every religion involves some sort of spirit possession. In some places and times it has high status and is encouraged, in others it is characterised as 'devil worship' and forbidden.

In yet others, as in Britain today, it seems to persist only on the margins, the province of the charlatan, the insane or the 'B' movie. And yet as we talked to people interested in taking part in this project, we found very few who had no experience of 'the spirit plane', if not directly then through a close relative, usually an aunt ('We never believed those things, but our Aunty Eth . . .'). The imagery of possession abounds in the language: 'I don't know what got into me', 'I was beside myself', 'She is very self-possessed'.

The spirits that are believed to possess human bodies in order to speak to the living may be good or evil. They may be ancestral spirits who advise and heal, or they may be the unquiet dead, spirits of the murdered or childless who return to take revenge for their unhappy lives.

Around the idea of possession an endless battle is waged. Direct contact with the divine is a source of power. In some societies it is the exclusive privilege of priests. In others it is believed that any good person may be chosen by a spirit as the body it inhabits. In societies where the state claims to rule with 'the mandate of heaven', to become possessed by a god or a spirit may be a means of challenging the state.

The Bacchae tells how the god Dionysos brought a new ecstatic religion to the city of Thebes and how those who at first refused to believe that man could be as a god were punished with too much ecstasy. Many religious movements begin as small ecstatic cults in opposition to the established church. As they gain authority so ecstasy dies away and bureaucracy takes over. In the eighteenth century, Methodists became possessed and spoke in tongues. No longer.

But we were interested in other forms of possession as well, possession by forces within as well as without: by memory, by fear, by anxiety, by habit. We chose to see possession as any form of behaviour that is not entirely under one's own control, because of alcohol, because of love, or because an old-established pattern has re-asserted itself allowing the past, either personal or general, to speak directly to the present. (Why are you violent? 'I come from a violent family. My father always hit me.')

A Mouthful of Birds tells the stories of seven possessed people. Possession may be an act of resistance; it is also an abandonment of control. Our new play, which began with *The Bacchae*, is itself possessed by it. Spirits of the murdered and the unquiet dead speak through our invented characters, but they do not overwhelm them.

At the end of *The Bacchae*, Agave, having killed her son in a surfeit of ecstasy, comes back down the mountain to the city. For our Agave this is a moment not to abandon herself to the bureaucratic powers of the state, but to fight to take back control.

DAVID LAN
Autumn 1986

JOINT STOCK THEATRE GROUP

Joint Stock Theatre Group was founded in 1974. Directors William Gaskill and Max Stafford-Clark and writer David Hare wanted to create an environment in which they had greater control over working methods and where they could extend the rehearsal period. This led to the ideas of an extended workshop period and of genuine collaboration between actor, director and writer. A company will spend three or four weeks doing research and improvisation around an idea, usually, though by no means always, proposed by a writer/director team. Then, traditionally, there is a gap in which the company splits up and the writer gets to work on the play. *A Mouthful of Birds* marks a departure from routine as the entire company have worked together for an unbroken twelve-week period with script being produced daily by the writers, and workshops leading directly into rehearsals.

The *Joint Stock Book*, an official biography of the company edited by Rob Ritchie will be published by Methuen London Ltd in January 1987. The book includes a full, illustrated chronology of all the productions since the Group was founded in 1974, and diverse contributions from members past and present. It aims to explain the controversial 'method', to chronicle the work itself, and to draw on the experiences and memories of the wide range of theatre practitioners who have participated in Joint Stock since its inception. The following extracts are taken from pieces by Tony Rohr, on *Epsom Downs*, Caryl Churchill, on *Light Shining in Buckinghamshire*, and Max Stafford-Clark.

Tony Rohr (actor)
Epsom Downs

I was a busker, a bookie, a trainer and the race course in *Epsom Downs* – the last in a green suit with a piece of artificial grass in my hand, smoking a cigarette in a long elegant holder. I also played a horse. I knew a lot about horses. When the company spent a day at the Derby I backed the winner at 6 to 1 – Lester Piggot on The Minstrel. Playing a horse was not quite so easy. At an early rehearsal, Howard Brenton insisted the actors cast as horses should be naked. Not stripped to the waist, or wearing a jockstrap but completely starkers. 'A horse is a naked animal,' he said, trying to sound reasonable. Bill thought it a wonderful theatrical image. (Max was directing the show.) When it came to the photo call the press were asked not to use any full length shots of the scenes with the horses. We didn't want the wrong kind of publicity or to ruin the moment in the show. This was Joint Stock after all. As soon as I appeared in my leather harness, the cameras clicked, the tabloids shuffled towards the stage. But, as good as their word, all the photos that appeared in the papers after the first night were cut off at the waist. Except, that is, for those that turned up in a little-known French magazine, a copy of which I was sent under plain cover some years later. Inside, between an article entitled 'Les femmes sont-elles excitées par l'idée du viol?' (Answer: 'Oui') and an ad for some kind of equipment, were the horse shots from Epsom Downs – full length, un-cropped, un-retouched.

Caryl Churchill (writer)
Light Shining in Buckinghamshire

There was reading and a wallchart; talking about ourselves; and all kinds of things mainly thought up by Max. I'd never seen an exercise or improvisation before and was as thrilled as a child at a pantomime. Each actor had to draw from a lucky dip of Bible texts and get up at once and preach, urging some extraordinary course of action justified from the Bible: 'Suffer little children to come unto me' became an impassioned plea to lay children in the street and run them over with a steamroller. They drew cards, one of which you meant you were eccentric to the power of that number, and then improvised a public place – a department store, a doctor's waiting room – till it gradually became clear who it was, how they were breaking conventions, how the others reacted. A word in the notebook conjures up half a day's work: 'Songs' – Colin Sell teaching the actors to sing psalms; 'Dives and Lazarus' – we tried acting out parables; 'vagrants' – the actors went out and observed tramps in the street and brought back what they had seen. Already on the third day I find, 'Talked to M – possibly quaker meeting as setting?' and that idea stayed after the workshop. One day we had a prayer meeting where everyone had to speak; someone wanted to eat an apple but Max made him pass it round and everyone had to say something about it; the last person didn't say anything but bit into it; and that ended up in the play. I condensed the Putney Debates so we could read them, and eventually, far shorter again, they went into the play. In a folder I find a scenario I wrote for a day's work: a character for each actor with a speech from before the war, a summary of what happened to them and what their attitude should be at an improvised prayer meeting, and how they ended up at the restoration. This before-during-after idea was something I took forward into the writing. There were improvisations about real people too, Coppe, Clarkson and the man who ate grass.

Next the nine-week writing time. Looking at the forgotten notebooks I can catch for a moment the excitement of being so crammed with ideas and seizing on structure, characters, incidents that might contain them. Colin and I were working fairly separately, though agreed on a before-during-after shape, something dark, ugly and mean.

Max Stafford-Clark (director)
Notes

What is Joint Stock? Many meetings and conversations concerned themselves with this question. It became our hardy perennial. When new members of the company opened it up the old hands groaned. The following extracts are from my own notes of company meetings held during 1977, the year of the permanent ensemble.

Friday, 5 March 1977. St Gabriel's Parish Hall. Twenty-two people at mammoth policy meeting. Eighteen wear jeans, four do not.

Pip Donaghy: We all need to fanshen. He talks very emotionally and we are all a little embarassed. Joint Stock must fanshen. I stay looking down and don't want to meet people's eyes.

Simon Callow: The personality of Joint Stock has come from the directors. We must appraise that. But he only offers in exchange that we should 'try to produce theatrical work of a very high quality'.

Gillian Barge: 'Other people can have the bright ideas which I can then support and get my energy from that.'

Howard Brenton: Commends our intense social observation. 'Having watched that policeman bleed all over the floor for three hours (A superintendent from the Met had come to the *Mad World* workshop) the question was asked can we do him?'

Will Knightley: 'What we tried to do with *Yesterday's News* was to arrive at a consensus without the guidance of a clear political point of view which had been provided for us by the book of *Fanshen*.

Graham Cowley: 'I think it's my job to like the shows.'

Jane Wood: 'I feel guilty about having a kid in this collective. You can't negate your whole life because you've joined a theatre group.'

Paul Freeman: 'If we were going to have a coherent political point of view it would have emerged by now.'

Barrie Keeffe: 'I think it's important to go from show to show and not be concerned about our public image . . . The real change is from verbal work to spectacular shows.'

Paul Freeman: 'What Bill and Simon both feel is that we lack a centre . . . a principle that binds us together.'

Bill Gaskill: 'We should be developing the work we want to do and putting it in front of the public . . . We must decide who is going to write the plays and who is going to direct them.'

Tom Wilkinson: 'Unless there's some kind of articulated credo the work will founder . . . Who do you wish to address?' Here comes the move towards populism again.

Cecily Hobbs: 'I don't think it's just a question of vulgaring it up.'

Bill Gaskill: Feels that our standard of work has dropped since *Fanshen* and that's because we have lost what we are doing it for, what centre we are operating from.

Tuesday, 9 March 1977. St Gabriel's Parish Hall. Thirteen people wearing jeans, one not.

Simon Callow: 'Well here we are again then, staring baffled and bemused into a circle.'

THE ROYAL COURT THEATRE CHALLENGE FUND

As the national theatre of new writing it is the Royal Court's particular role to produce challenging new work and maintain British theatre as the most exciting in the world. Once again we have a shortfall in funding that threatens the number of plays we can produce.

Last year, in recognition of our work, Joseph Papp, Producer of the Public Theatre in New York, challenged us to raise £50,000, which he matched with $50,000. We raised £55,000 – and put on a very successful year's work.

This year he has challenged us to raise the same amount again: to be matched by another $50,000. One of the ways in which we hope to raise the target sum is through the recently initiated Patronage and Sponsorship Scheme – aimed at both business and private sources.

● **For £1,000** you can be a Patron, and in return we will offer you four top price tickets for each show Upstairs and Down throughout the year. In addition we will entertain you and your guests before each show and during the interval. You will be given life membership of the Royal Court Theatre Society and your name will feature on the Challenge Fund Display in the Stalls Bar.

● **For £250** you can become a Sponsor, which entitles you to two top price tickets for a Preview or the First Night of each show Up and Down throughout the year and membership of the Theatre Society for five years.

● **For £50** you can be a Friend of the Royal Court and we will give you two tickets for a Preview of every Main House show throughout the year.

Patrons
Henny Gestetner OBE, Roland Joffe, Martin Sheen

Sponsors
Linda Bassett Michael Codron Anne Devlin David Kleeman London Arts Discovery Tours Lesley Manville Patricia Marmont Debbie McWilliams, The Casting Company Gary Oldman Greville Poke Margaret Ramsay Sir Dermot de Trafford

Friends
John Arthur Glen Berelowitz & Lindsey Stevens Jim Broadbent Paul Brooke Ralph Brown Angela Coles Jeremy Conway Lou Coulson Alan David Adrian Dunbar Jan Evans, Evans & Reiss John Evans & Judith Fenn Trevor Eve Kenneth Ewing, Fraser & Dunlop Scripts Ltd Kate Feast Gilly Fraser David Gant Kerry Gardner Jonathan Gems Sharon Hamper, Hamper Neafsey Associates Jocelyn Herbert Derek Hornby Dusty Hughes Kenny Ireland J C & M E Jaqua Paul Jesson Sheila Lemon Suzie Mackenzie Philip McDonald Marina Martin Richard O'Brien Stephen Oliver Gary Olsen Harold Pinter Jane Rayne Alan Rickman A J Sayers Roxanne Shafer Sir Clive Sinclair Richard Stone Nigel Terry Mary Trevelyan Tracey Ullman Maureen Vincent, Fraser & Dunlop Ltd Julian Wadham Julie Walters Sarah Wheatland

And the companies of *The Normal Heart Road Ourselves Alone*

Financially assisted by the Royal Borough of Kensington and Chelsea

COMING NEXT IN THE
THEATRE UPSTAIRS 01-730 2254

From 20 November

BYRTHRITE by Sarah Daniels
Directed by Carole Hayman, designed by Jenny Tiramani, music by Jo-Anne Fraser

A tough, moving and humorous new play from the author of *Masterpieces*. *Byrthrite* is a drama with songs about reproductive technology, set in the 17th century. The group of women at the centre of the story are faced with the threat of the 'pricker' or Witchfinder General. They live in an age in which the profession of doctor was established, when women were hanged for the crime of midwifery.

'Women of our time are stronger than ever before,' the play says 'and yet persecuted worse at same time.'

From 23 January

PERDITION by Jim Allen
Directed by Ken Loach

A young woman journalist writes a pamphlet attacking the Jewish Councils, especially Dr Yaron, for collaborating with the Nazis during the war. Yaron sues her for libel, and this controversial new play follows the trial, setting out the arguments about one of the most heated and tragic conflicts in modern history. Without sensationalising or vulgarizing, author Jim Allen raises a series of powerful and complex questions about ethics and choices. What were the choices facing the Jews during the Holocaust – resistance or co-operation? When does co-operation become collaboration? How guilty were the Allies, the international Jewish community, the Zionist leadership and the Jews in Hungary themselves?

From 13 March

THE EMPEROR by Ryszard Kapuściński
The Emperor by Ryszard Kapuściński is an analysis of the last days of Haile Selassie. The King of Kings was left in isolation in the Old Palace. One by one his retainers fled. Only the venerable Servants of the Foot-stool remained. Nothing was altered. The corridors were calm, the leopards were fed. Sprinklers rotated on the lawn. Just the royal gates were locked from the outside. Michael Hastings and Jonathan Miller have completed a workshop on this world famous book. They hope to present a staged version at the Theatre Upstairs in March.

FOR THE ROYAL COURT THEATRE

Direction

Artistic Director	MAX STAFFORD-CLARK
Director/Theatre Upstairs	SIMON CURTIS
Associate Directors	CAROLE HAYMAN*
	DAVID HAYMAN*
	ROB RITCHIE*
Trainee Director	HETTIE MACDONALD
Senior Script Associate	MICHAEL HASTINGS*
Casting Director	SERENA HILL
Associate Writer	TIMBERLAKE WERTENBAKER*
Thames TV Writer-in-Residence	JIM CARTWRIGHT*

Production

Production Manager	ALISON RITCHIE
Technical Manager/Theatre Upstairs	CHRIS BAGUST
Chief Electrician	CHRISTOPHER TOULMIN
Deputy Chief Electrician	ACE McCARRON
Electrician	COLIN ROXBOROUGH*
Sound Designer	CHRISTOPHER SHUTT
Master Carpenter	CHRIS HARDING-ROBERTS
Deputy Carpenter	JOHN BURGESS
Wardrobe Supervisor	JENNIFER COOK
Wardrobe Assistant	CATHIE SKILBECK

Administration

General Manager	JOSEPHINE BEDDOE
Membership Secretary	SUSIE BREAKELL
Literary Secretary	JODY ORGIAS*
General Manager's Secretary	ROSE DEW*
Financial Administrator	FREYA PINSENT
Financial Assistant	PAULINE DJEMAL
Press & Publicity Manager	SHARON KEAN
Press & Publicity/Theatre Upstairs	NATASHA HARVEY
House Manager	TOBY WHALE
Assistant House Manager	CHRISTOPHER MILLARD
Box Office Manager	CHRISTOPHER PEARCY
Box Office Assistants	KEITH SHAND
	PAT GIBBONS
Stage Door/Telephonist	SALLY HARRIS*
Cleaners	EILEEN CHAPMAN
	IVY JONES*
	MARIE TOOMEY*
Maintenance	JOHN LORRIGIO*
Evening Stage Door	TYRONE LUCAS*
Head Usher	VALERIE GABBIDON*
Firemen	WILFRED BARTLETT*
	PAUL KLEINMANN*

Young People's Theatre
Director   ELYSE DODGSON
Administrator   CARIN MISTRY
Schools and Community Liaison Worker   MARK HOLNESS
Writer-in-Residence   HANIF KUREISHI*

Council: Chairman Matthew Evans, Stuart Burge CBE, Anthony C Burton, Caryl Churchill, Harriet Cruickshank, Simon Curtis, Allan Davis, David Lloyd Davis, Robert Fox, William Gaskill, Mrs Henny Gestetner OBE, Derek Granger, David Hare, Jocelyn Herbert, David Kleeman, Sonia Melchett, Joan Plowright CBE, Greville Poke, Jane Rayne, Alison Ritchie, Toby Whale, Sir Hugh Willatt.

*Part-time staff

BECOME A MEMBER OF THE ROYAL COURT THEATRE SOCIETY

and have the best seat in the House for only £2.50 for any preview in the main theatre and the Theatre Upstairs.
Membership will cost you only £7.50 a year.
For this you will get
• Free advance information about the plays at the Royal Court and the Theatre Upstairs
• Exclusive priority booking
• Special offers with every show

Join Now!
Cheque/P.O. for £7.50 made payable to Royal Court Theatre Society, c/o Susie Breakell.

CAST BIOGRAPHIES

AMELDA BROWN

Amelda trained at RADA, where she won the Ronson Prize and Silver Medal. Theatre credits include GIRL TALK at Soho Poly; CHILD'S PLAY at the Belgrade, Coventry; TOP GIRLS at Leicester Haymarket and FALKLAND SOUND, again at Coventry. She has worked with Joint Stock on three previous productions; she was part of the original FEN cast and went to the Britain Salutes New York Festival in 1983. She was also in THE POWER OF THE DOG and FIRE IN THE LAKE, the latter directed by Les Waters. Last year she played Tanzi in TRAFFORD TANZI at the Octagon, Bolton. TV and film credits include SHERLOCK HOLMES: THE BLUE CARBUNCLE for Granada and AN ENGLISH CHRISTMAS for Channel 4. She is soon to be seen as Fanny in the film LITTLE DORRIT with Alec Guiness and Derek Jacobi and in the new John Boorman film HOPE AND GLORY.

CHRISTIAN BURGESS

After training at Guildhall, Christian appeared in the first three productions of Common Stock Theatre Company. He was a founder member of Shared Experience in 1975, appearing in the ARABIAN NIGHTS TRILOGY and recently THE THREE SISTERS playing Solyony. This production is his third with Joint Stock, after THE RAGGED TROUSERED PHILANTHROPISTS and AN OPTIMISTIC THRUST, both directed by Bill Gaskill. Other theatre credits include A FAIR QUARREL at the National Theatre, ANTHONY AND CLEOPATRA at the Shaw, ANIMAL at the Traverse, Edinburgh, TOUCH AND GO at Riverside. Television includes RACHEL IN DANGER and HANDS for Thames and REAL LIVE AUDIENCE, RABBIT DAY PIE, GOING GENTLY and HARD TRAVELLING for the BBC. Christian also spent four years working in London and New York, producing and promoting the graphic works of artists including Jasper Johns, David Hockney, Frank Stella and Howard Hodgkin.

DONA CROLL

Dona comes from Birmingham and trained there. She has worked extensively in Rep throughout the country with seasons at Birmingham Rep, Leicester, Sheffield, etc. Recent theatre credits include Berinthia in THE RELAPSE at the Lyric, Hammersmith, Damarisk in POLLY, on tour with Cambridge Theatre Company and The Serpent in BACK TO METHUSELAH, also with CTC. She played Dorcas in GOLDEN GIRLS at Leeds Playhouse followed by two plays at the Royal Court Theatre Upstairs – BASIN and GOD'S SECOND IN COMMAND. Her television appearances include BBC's ANGELS, SARAH AND LOUISE, THE GENTLE TOUCH, THE BOYS FROM THE BLACK STUFF, COME TO MECCA, THE NATION'S HEALTH, BLACK SILK and EBONY. She has also been a presenter on the 6 O'CLOCK SHOW for LWT and BLACK AND WHITE AND READ ALL OVER, a book programme for Channel 4.

PHILIPPE GIRAUDEAU

Philippe comes from La Rochelle where he trained as a dancer. He has worked as a professional dancer in France before joining London Contemporary Dance where he met Siobhan Davies, which led him to work with Second Stride and Ian Spink. As a dancer he has also appeared with Mantis and on television and films. His English credits also include SECRET GARDENS, I.Q. OF 4 and THE PRINCESS OF CLEVES in which he played the Duc de Nemours, all at the ICA, and the national tour of SONG AND DANCE. He recently worked with Ian Spink in BOSENDORFER WALTZES and appeared on a French television programme with his brother with whom he filmed LE CRI DU SILENCE.

STEPHEN GOFF

Born in Newcastle upon Tyne in 1953 Stephen played rugby for Northumberland Schools and football for Newcastle United Juniors. On leaving school he studied PE at Doncaster College for one year and then worked for two years in Newcastle Fruit Market. Subsequent jobs included waiter, baker's roundsman and insurance salesman. In 1977 he enrolled on the BA course at the Laban Centre for Movement and Dance and graduated in 1980 with First Class Honours. He then did research for the Gulbenkian Foundation and wrote on dance for Time Out and Dance Theatre Journal. Dance credits include performances with Michael Clark and Dancers and Mantis Dance Company and productions choreographed by Ian Spink for Scottish Opera and Opera North. He collaborated successfully with sculptor Andrew Golding on their performance piece LOGS AND HEADS and recently worked with Paul Clayden on a duo performance DEADLINING. In 1981 he won the New Choreographers Award Scheme with ANNA BLUME a solo for Annelis Stoffel and his own solo work work includes MAN ON (1982), TRANWELL WOODS (1983) and CAMEL RIDE (1985).

TRICIA KELLY

Tricia began her career as an ASM at Liverpool Everyman, then spent three years with Perspectives Theatre working in schools and community venues. Work followed with numerous companies including 7:84, Red Ladder, Woman's Theatre Group, Chester Gateway, Soho Poly and Croydon Warehouse. She appeared in Joint Stock's highly acclaimed FEN which toured nationally and played to packed houses at Joe Papp's Public Theater, New York. Most recent work includes DEADLINES, by Stephen Wakelam, also for Joint Stock (national tour/Royal Court), TOP GIRLS (Lancaster), GOD'S WONDERFUL RAILWAY (Bristol Old Vic), BEAUTY AND THE BEAST (Liverpool Playhouse/The Old Vic) and THE COUNTRY WIFE (Coventry). Recent TV includes IN SICKNESS AND IN HEALTH and THIS IS HISTORY, GRAN, both for the BBC.

VIVIENNE ROCHESTER

Vivienne trained in Drama, English and Dance in Manchester and won scholarships to the London School of Contemporary Dance and the Alvin Ailey School, New York. She has since worked as both an actress and a dancer; her theatre work includes leading roles as Judy in MONEY TO LIVE, Winnie in BLUES FOR RAILTON and Miss Brandon in SMILE ORANGE. She appeared as Miss B in PIRATE PRINCESS and was in TOUISSANT at the Coliseum. She was a soloist with MAAS Movers and Dance Theatre Workshop, New York and a principal with English Dance Theatre and the Chamber Dance Theatre. Her TV credits include GENTLE TOUCH for LWT, LATE STARTER, KILLING TIME, BASIN and SOME DRINKS AND GOOD TIMES for the BBC and the Channel 4 series STREETS AHEAD. She has also worked on several radio plays, three videos and two films.

CARYL CHURCHILL

Caryl Churchill has written for TV, radio and the theatre. Her stage plays include OWNERS, OBJECTIONS TO SEX AND VIOLENCE, TRAPS, TOP GIRLS (Royal Court), VINEGAR TOM (Monstrous Regiment), SOFTCOPS (RSC), and for Joint Stock LIGHT SHINING IN BUCKINGHAMSHIRE, CLOUD NINE and FEN. CLOUD NINE, TOP GIRLS and FEN all had successful runs in New York, CLOUD NINE playing for over two years. Both CLOUD NINE and TOP GIRLS won OBIES. She has worked with Les Waters before on CLOUD NINE, THREE MORE SLEEPLESS NIGHTS (Soho Poly) and FEN.

DAVID LAN
David Lan's first play PAINTING A WALL was performed at the Almost Free
Theatre in 1974. This was followed by three plays at the Royal Court Theatre
Upstairs: BIRD CHILD, PARADISE and THE WINTER DANCERS which
won the 1977 John Whiting award. RED EARTH was produced at the ICA in
1978. SERGEANT OLA AND HIS FOLLOWERS, on the Royal Court main
stage in 1979, won the George Orwell Memorial Award, and in 1986 FLIGHT
was produced by the RSC at the Other Place. His TV film THE SUNDAY
JUDGE was shown on BBC 2 last year and his book GUNS AND RAIN, an
anthropological study of spirit mediums and guerrillas in Zimbabwe, was
published last autumn.

IAN SPINK
Born in Australia, Ian danced with the Australian Ballet and the Australian
Dance Theatre and Dance Company NSW for several years before coming to
England in 1977. Initially he formed his own company, the Ian Spink Group,
which performed experimental works such as 26 SOLOS and DE GAS (both of
which combined dance with theatre) and SOME FUGUES and CANTA. Since
1981 Ian has co-founded and choreographed with Second Stride where his shows,
all collaborations with designer Antony McDonald and composer Orlando
Gough, have been NEW TACTICS, FURTHER AND FURTHER INTO
NIGHT and BOSENDORFER WALTZES. Ian's opera and theatre work
include MAZEPPA for ENO, ORLANDO for Scottish Opera and
MIDSUMMER MARRIAGE for Opera North. At the ICA he co-directed
WAR CRIMES and SECRET GARDENS; he worked on movement for the
RSC's touring production of THE CRUCIBLE and THE WINTER'S TALE and
with The Fires of London on VESALLII ICONES. Ian's work was seen on
Channel 4's first dance season and on the BBC's Omnibus. Most recently Ian
choreographed MERCURE for Ballet Rambert.

LES WATERS
Les has worked extensively at the Royal Court Theatre. His many productions
there include MARIE AND BRUCE by Wallace Shawn, SEDUCED by Sam
Shepard, ABEL'S SISTER by Timberlake Wertenbaker, NOT QUITE
JERUSALEM by Paul Kember and INSIGNIFICANCE by Terry Johnson. In
1982 he directed FEN by Caryl Churchill for Joint Stock Theatre Group. FEN
toured nationally, played the Almeida and the Royal Court and was a great
success at the Public Theater, New York. In 1984 Les returned to New York to
direct FEN with an American cast. Other productions include FUGUE by Rona
Munro at the Traverse, Edinburgh, THREE MORE SLEEPLESS NIGHTS by
Caryl Churchill at Soho Poly, LOOSE ENDS by Michael Weller at Hampstead
Theatre Club, FIRE IN THE LAKE by Karim Alrawi for Joint Stock,
SALONIKA by Louise Page and THE SEAGULL by Anton Chekhov, both for
Liverpool Playhouse and an acclaimed production of RUM AND COKE by
Keith Reddin at the Public Theater, New York. Future projects include shows in
Washington and Minneapolis.

ANNIE SMART

Annie took a degree in drama at Manchester University and the theatre design course at ENO. She has worked extensively throughout Britain and amongst her recent credits were Resident Designer at Leicester Haymarket Studio where she designed Molière's GEORGE DANDIN, Euripides' MEDEA, Buchner's WOYZECK and Ionesco's BALD PRIMA DONNA. She has worked for Joint Stock twice before, on FEN which she was later asked to recreate in New York and Dusseldorf and on FIRE IN THE LAKE. For the last year she has been head of Design at Liverpool Playhouse where her shows have included MISS JULIE, BEAUTY AND THE BEAST, which transferred to the Old Vic, and most recently GIMME SHELTER by Barrie Keeffe.

RICK FISHER

Originally from the United States, Rick has been working in British Theatre for ten years. His credits include GERTRUDE STEIN AND A COMPANION at the Bush and Hampstead Theatre and A BOLT OUT OF THE BLUE at the Almeida Theatre. Operas by Handel, Salieri, Monteverdi and Paisiello at Musica Nel Chiostro, Batignano, Italy, Flann O'Brien's HARD LIFE at the Tricycle Theatre and Rossini's CINDERELLA for the English Touring Opera. He recently lit Les Water's production of THE SEAGULL at Liverpool Playhouse. Rick is a founding member of That's Not It Theatre Company and has just finished a short stint with SPITTING IMAGE for Central TV.

Notes

1. Sometimes one character starts to speak before another has finished. The point of overlap is indicated by a slash [/].

2. The movement pieces have been described very briefly in the text. Anyone wishing to perform the play should obtain a video showing the choreography by Ian Spink from Harriet Cruickshank, 97 Old South Lambeth Road, London SW8 1XU.

3. In the original production the play was set on two levels of a dilapidated house. The set remained throughout. The action was continuous.

ACT ONE

PART ONE

1. DIONYSOS dances.

He is played by a man. He wears a white petticoat.

Skinning a rabbit

LENA *and* ROY.
ROY *is holding a dead white rabbit.*

LENA (*to audience*): Look at the hole in its stomach.
  (*To* ROY:) I couldn't possibly.

ROY. I'll skin it for you.

LENA. Look at its face.

ROY. My grandmother used to cook them with prunes.

LENA. Do you know how to skin it?

ROY. I've shot rabbits.

LENA. Look at the hole in its stomach.

ROY. It's like chicken.

LENA. It's so white. All right. If you do it all.

ROY. You soak the prunes.

2. Telephone

MARCIA *is operating a switchboard.*

MARCIA (*to audience*). In fact I am desperate.
  (*On telephone*). Continental Lingerie, hold the line.
  Yes, sir? Sir, I am busy.
  Continental Lingerie, hold the line.
  Yes? Who? Putting you through.
  (*West Indian accent.*) You there? . . . so my boss asked me, had I ever been to the Ritz
  . . . Hang on a minute.
  Yes? Look, if this goes on –. It's your firm that suffers. Well, *I* care. I do.
  (*West Indian accent.*) You there? . . . so I told him straight, I said, quick as a flash . . .

COLIN *comes in.*
  Pause.

  Ooh, new trousers? Fit you ever so snug.

COLIN. My office. Now.

MARCIA. Get me a cup of tea, be a sweetie.

Continental Lingerie. I'm afraid you can't. He's having a meeting with a lady friend.

COLIN *gestures 'Who?'*
MARCIA *gestures 'You'.*
COLIN *gestures 'Me?'*

MARCIA. Yes, sir. But he won't want to speak to you. He told me himself he doesn't care what happens to the firm. He's only interested in –

COLIN *goes out.*

MARCIA. Putting you through.
(*West Indian accent.*) You there? . . . I'd have to be desperate to look at him. In fact I am desperate. Even so . . . Oh, hang on.
Continental Lingerie. Putting you through.

3. Weightlifting

DEREK *and two other men are doing weights*

DEREK (*to audience*). He thought he wasn't a man without a job.

MAN 1. How long since you worked?

DEREK. A while.

MAN 1. I've never worked.

Silence.

MAN 2. I'm going for an interview tomorrow.

MAN 1. What for?

MAN 2. They make biscuits.

MAN 1. Do you know about biscuits?

MAN 2. Seven years' experience of marketing. First-class degree in economics. I've eaten biscuits.

MAN 1. So we might not be seeing so much of you.

Pause.

MAN 2. I've had twenty-three interviews.

Silence.

DEREK. Seventeen months.

Silence.

MAN 2. Sometimes I think I'll go mad.

DEREK. No. I don't mind at all any more. I have activities. Swimming, karate, jogging, garden, weights. There's not enough hours in the day if you put your mind to it. My father couldn't. He thought he wasn't a man without a job. He died within six weeks. But there's no need.

Silence.

MAN 1. I can't imagine working.

4. Sleep

YVONNE, *an acupuncturist, is attending to* MR WOOD *who is lying down. She wears a white coat.*

YVONNE (*to audience*). What is it makes you so angry?
  (*To* MR WOOD.) Relax your arm. No, relax it. All right. Let's start at the top. Back. Relax your back. All the way down. There. Now shoulder. Let it go. Good. Elbow. Wrist. Fingers. All the joints. Let the tension flow away. That's it.

She inserts a needle.

Good. So, Mr Wood, tell me – what is it makes you so angry?

She inserts a needle.

You need to think about it so much? You haven't slept for a week, I give up my lunch break, you come in, your whole body's tense. There must be something winding you up.

She inserts a needle.

Good. Now your neck. Relaaax.

She inserts a needle.

So what is it?

MR WOOD. Gumminumminumminummi goo goo . . .

YVONNE. Mr Wood? How can I help you if you fall asleep? Mr Wood!

5. Profit

PAUL *and* MOTHER-IN-LAW *are playing chess.*

PAUL (*to audience*). That way we make more profit.

MOTHER-IN-LAW. I know you don't like me phoning the office. Mother-in-law.

PAUL. That's perfectly all right. If it's important.

MOTHER-IN-LAW. June wasn't home and I thought . . . I think I've got your queen.

PAUL. No.

MOTHER-IN-LAW. Ah.

  Pause.

So will you be coming to us for the weekend?

PAUL. If I bring some work.

  She moves.

MOTHER-IN-LAW. Check.

  He moves.

PAUL. Check.

MOTHER-IN-LAW. Could that be mate?

PAUL. I think so.

He picks up the telephone, dials.

First Berlin, then Boulogne.

He puts the telephone down.

MOTHER-IN-LAW. What?

PAUL. Fifty thousand tons of beef. We move them from Birmingham first to Berlin then to Boulogne. I was working it out.

MOTHER-IN-LAW. Unless my rook – no.

PAUL. That way we make more profit.

MOTHER-IN-LAW. You're very clever.

6. Angels

DAN, *a vicar. Three* WOMEN *in hats.* WOMAN 1 *has a bag of jumble.*

DAN (*to audience*). I don't believe God is necessarily male.

WOMAN 1. Where shall I put the jumble?

DAN. In the vestry.

WOMAN 2. Do you believe in angels?

WOMAN 3. But when it comes to the ordination of women, have we your support or not?

DAN. I don't believe God is necessarily male in the conventional . . . But I do think there's a time and a place . . . I entirely agree with the bishop when he –

WOMAN 2. Do you believe in angels?

DAN. I'm sorry?

7. Home

DOREEN *is standing some distance from* ED.

DOREEN (*to audience*). All I wanted was peace and quiet.
(*To* ED.) I never said I wouldn't come home.

ED. You didn't say nothing. You just ran, left me sitting on the bench like a fool.

DOREEN. All I wanted was peace and quiet. I found it.

ED. Sleeping by that canal, on that grass? And to scratch me and tear me. What for? I was searching five hours. Look, I'm still bleeding. Come here.

DOREEN. I was happy.

ED. I warned you what would happen if you ran off again.

DOREEN. What? What will happen? What?

Pause.

ED. Well, you had your day out all right.

DOREEN. Oh I did.

8. Excuses

i.

PAUL (*on telephone*). I'm sorry I can't make the conference. I've sprained my ankle.

MARCIA (*on telephone*). I can't come in, I've lost my voice.

YVONNE (*on telephone*). I'm afraid I have to cancel your appointment, I've hurt my hand.

DOREEN. I won't be in today, I'm seeing double.

DEREK. I can't go swimming this morning, I've got a hangover.

DAN. I really can't do the wedding, I've got earache.

LENA. I can't come to tea, I've cut my finger.

ii.

DEREK. I can't come to the pub tonight, my dog's gone missing.

LENA. I can't distribute the leaflets, there's a power cut.

MARCIA. I can't see you tonight, my car's broken down.

YVONNE. I can't come to the funeral, the trains have been cancelled.

DAN. I can't visit the old people, my mother's turned up.

DOREEN. I know it's my turn to collect them but the kitchen's flooded.

PAUL. I can't fly to Rome. My cousin has died.

iii.

LENA. I can't come in for a perm, my sister's been kidnapped.

YVONNE. I can't go to the disco, the army's closed off the street.

DOREEN. I can't come to dinner, there's a bull in the garden.

DEREK. I can't play tonight, my house has blown down.

DAN. I can't see the bishop, the vestry's on fire.

PAUL. I can't meet the deadline. The chairman's been struck by lightning.

MARCIA. I'll have to see the dentist another time, my aunt's gone crazy.

LENA. So I just stayed in all day.

PART TWO

9. Psychic Attack

LENA (*to audience*). Look at the hole in its stomach.

ROY. LENA. SPIRIT.
The SPIRIT is seen and heard only by LENA.
Breakfast time on four successive days.

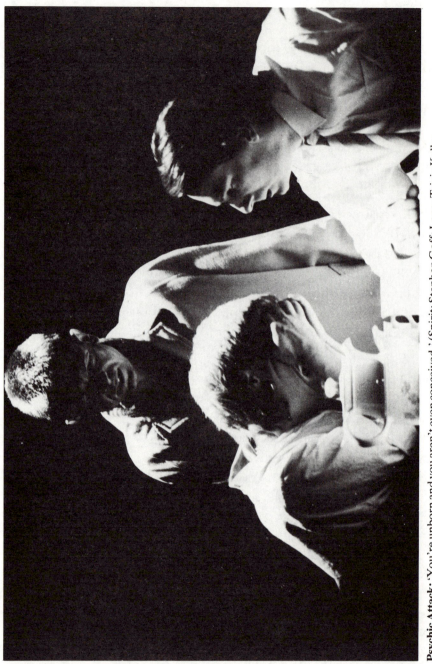

Psychic Attack: 'You're unborn and you aren't even conceived.' (Spirit: Stephen Goff; Lena: Tricia Kelly; Roy: Christian Burgess)

i.

LENA *sets the table.* ROY *comes in.*

ROY. So at the light he gets level again and
I don't look at him but he knows and I
know that one of us is going to be in
trouble because over the crossing it's got
to be single lane because there's cars
parked. And I'm on the outside so I've
every right but I know/ from what he's   SPIRIT. teapot teapot teapot teapot.
done already that he's going to cut in if he
possibly can and he knows that I'm going
to keep him out and with any luck he'll get
smashed on the parked cars. I can see
without looking the kind of person he is
and it's a kind I don't like and will not put
up with, the whole way he sat there
with his elbow out the window,/ I thought   elbow out the window
to myself I'll have that elbow off,   elbow out the window
I'll have that elbow right off.   elbow out the window
So the minute the lights change the
other side – *and* there's a stupid
bastard/ crossing the other way only   stupid bastard stupid bastard
gets through on the red – and we're both   stupid bastard
off with a hell of a screech and he's got a
slight edge because pure and simple it's a
faster car, nothing to do with his driving,
it's a new car, but I've got my foot hard
down and I not only get ahead but I swing
out a bit to my left before I swing in
round the back of the parked cars/ and   LENA. Do you want some more toast?
he's had to pull away and he's got to brake
hard and he just catches me on the
bumper and he hits the island and lucky
for him there's no kiddy waiting to cross
the road. And I go up the street and down
the next turning because he's going to
come after me but I'm off down the back
doubles and I reckon I showed him.

ROY *goes.*

Lena and Spirit – Transformations

*He is a frog. She approaches threateningly as a snake. He seizes her arm and becomes a lover.
She responds but as he embraces her he becomes an animal and attacks the back of her neck.
She puts him down to crawl and he becomes a train. As he chugs under the table she blocks the
tunnel with a chair and he rolls out as a threatening bird. She becomes a baby bird asking to be
fed and he feeds her. As he goes to get more food she becomes a panther, knocks him to the
ground and starts to eat him. After a moment he leaps up with a fierce roar. She goes into the
next scene.*

ii.

LENA *sets the table.* ROY *comes in.*

ROY. Don't forget to phone your mother.

SPIRIT. You're useless. Can't wipe your own bum. Useless baby.

ROY. Remind me to get a light bulb.

You're going to be unborn. You are unborn. You're not conceived. Your parents never met. Your parents/ were never born. Your parents were never conceived. Your grandparents never met. That's how useless you are.

LENA. I better go to the launderette today.

ROY. The plumber's coming on Thursday.

LENA. I think I'll take Sally to the park.

Because you don't stand up to him. He's disgusting. He fills the whole/ room up.

His hair smells. His eyes have got yellow in the corners. His ears have got hairs on. His nose has got big pores and the nostrils are too big and full of hair and snot and he snores/ and snorts. His teeth are yellow. His tongue's yellow. His mouth tastes of shit because it's directly connected to his arsehole.

LENA. Can we talk about a holiday?

LENA. Am I putting on weight?

ROY. I'm not made of money you know.

LENA. Don't forget to get a lightbulb.

ROY. Mind you I'd like a break.

LENA. Sure you don't want an egg?

The order is to kill the baby. The order is to kill the baby. Because the baby is directly/ connected to him. The baby is directly connected to you. The baby is directly connected to me./ When you kill the baby you'll be free of him. You'll be free of yourself. You'll be free of me. That's why you're going to kill the baby.

ROY. No.

ROY *goes.* LENA *and* SPIRIT *struggle.* LENA *finally gets the* SPIRIT *down and leaves him lying still as she goes into the next scene. After a moment he gets up and goes into the scene.*

iii.

LENA *sets the table.* ROY *comes in.*

ROY. So what I'm going to do is say to him/ straight out, what about that twenty pounds you owe me? Because it's three weeks, it's over three weeks, it was the Sunday after the Saturday Arsenal beat Liverpool at home. He thinks he can let it slide and I won't do that. What about that twenty pounds you owe me? That's the best way.

SPIRIT. Teapot. Cup. Cup. Is that a cup? You don't know do you because you're useless, you're not born, you're not conceived of, this house was never built.

ROY. So what was the matter with you
last night?

LENA. I don't know what you mean.

ROY. What do you mean you don't know
what I mean?

They both start speaking at once.

ROY. Have you gone off me?
I don't need to stick around where
I'm not wanted.

LENA. Of course you're wanted.

ROY. Are you trying to tell me/ there's
someone else because just tell me.

LENA. There's nobody./ Please don't.
I love you.

ROY. Because I'm not bothered.

LENA. Please don't, I really/ need you,
I do need you. Please, come on,/ I was
tired last night.

ROY. I don't know what the idea is./ I
think you're having me on.

LENA. I'm not, I'm really – Please
please please.

ROY. All right. All right. We'll see how
we go.

ROY. So what I'm going to do/ is say to
him straight out what about that
twenty pounds you owe me. Because it's
three weeks.

He continues speech as above but silently.

ROY (*aloud again*). Twenty pounds you
owe me, that's the best way.

LENA. All right.

The universe will go forward again
when you kill the baby. Then he/
won't fill up all the space. Then
you might get born. Then I'll stop talking
and go away because then you'll have
done what you should and you won't be
useless.

His eyes have got red lines. His
fingernails have got muck under./ The
hairs in his arse are stuck together.
His cock's got goo coming out. His feet
are full of black cracks.

When he breathes it takes your breath
away.

He swallows the air.
That's why you don't exist.

The solution is to kill the baby.
Hold the baby under the water.

Because you're a baby and you're
unborn and you aren't even conceived.

You should be sick on his hair. You
should piss in his tea. You should rub
blood on his teeth. You should shit on his
eyes. You should hold the baby under
the water.

Then I'll go away. When you've
killed the baby it's going to be quiet.

The SPIRIT *climbs onto* ROY's *back and pushes him down onto the table.* LENA *washes
a shawl in a baby bath.*

iv.

LENA *returns to the table.*

ROY. So I'll phone up and book today. I
could really do with a break myself. I
know how much you've been wanting to

go away.

LENA. I have to talk to you.
   I think if you go to the bathroom.
   I think Sally's drowned.

ROY. What did you say?
   What did you say?

   ROY *keeps repeating the same gesture and words.*

LENA. It wasn't me that did it.

ROY. What did you say?

SPIRIT. Teapot teapot teapot teapot.

LENA. I thought you'd gone.
   You said you'd go away.

You're unborn. His hair smells.

ROY. What did you say?

LENA. I poured the teapot and blood
   came out.

10. Possession

DIONYSOS *appears to* DOREEN.
DOREEN *is possessed by* AGAVE.

AGAVE. I put my foot against its side and tore out its shoulder. I broke open its ribs.

11. Fruit ballet

Whole company as their main characters.
This dance consists of a series of movements mainly derived from eating fruit. It emphasises the sensuous pleasures of eating and the terrors of being torn up.

12. Possession

DIONYSOS *appears to* DEREK.
DEREK *is possessed by* PENTHEUS.

DEREK. She put her foot against my side and tore out my shoulder. They broke open my ribs.

13. Baron Sunday

MARCIA (*to audience*). In fact I am desperate.

MARCIA*'s basement and then* DECIMA*'s room in north London.*
In MARCIA*'s basement: two chairs (A1 & A2) on either side of a table, a third chair (A3) a short way behind and to the side of one of the others.*
A repeat of this arrangement of tables and chair stands to the left – B1, B2, B3.

Fruit Ballet. (Marjorie Yates, Stephen Goff, Tricia Kelly, Christian Burgess)

Fruit Ballet. (Stephen Goff *in foreground*, Tricia Kelly, Christian Burgess)

Fruit Ballet. Dona Croll (*in foreground*), Vivienne Rochester, Philippe Giraudeau)

i.

Table A has a white table cloth and a small glass vase of flowers.
MARCIA, a Trinidadian medium in her mid-thirties, sits on chair A1.
On A2, opposite MARCIA, sits DECIMA a younger Trinidadian woman.
SYBIL, a spirit from the white upper-middle classes, sits on chair B3.
When MARCIA speaks as the spirit, she uses a very deep voice.

DECIMA. Who are you?

Pause.

DECIMA. If you don' say something soon, Marcia, I'm gonna ask my money back. Who are you?

Pause.

OK. I got shoppin' a do, I got my mama's laundry, I got plenty, plenty.

Pause.

DECIMA. Why'd you make me give you all a' my ten p's? Listen, m'dear, the truth is I saved those ten p's for the launderette. I don' know what got into me to give you all a' them. You hear me? Marcia? Give me back my ten p's, I'll go down the launderette an' come try again nex' week. It ain' no shame if you can' do it one time. Marcia, girl? You hear me?

MARCIA. Baron Sunday.

DECIMA. You said?

MARCIA. This is Baron Sunday talkin' to you. Ask.

DECIMA. Where is the bracelet was stole from me?

Pause.

MARCIA. In purgatory.

DECIMA. You said? My bracelet? Purgatory? What for? It weren't worth hardly nothing. C'mon, Marce. Give me the ten p's, let me get on down the launderette.

MARCIA. The one who thiefed the bracelet, that's the one's in purgatory. The penalty to break god's law – hm – death.

DECIMA. And the bracelet?

MARCIA. Ha ha ha ha.

DECIMA. I love that bracelet. Uncle Short Plank sent it all the way for me.

MARCIA. Ha ha ha ha ha.

SYBIL. You can't tell her where it is. Can you?

Pause.

MARCIA. Where is it? Where? (*Own voice.*) Go down the launderette. Try again nex' week.

DECIMA goes out.

ii.

MARCIA *stands and moves towards table B. She hesitates, retreats to A1, sits.*

SYBIL. You come to this place. Why not? You try to pack your powers in your knapsack. They're fond of you. They like to help. They come. They stay awhile. They go. Of course they do. What are you left with? What? But you have such skill. Experience. Technique. I've been waiting and waiting.

MARCIA (*own voice*). Who are you?

Pause.

MARCIA (*with defiance*). Baron Sunday betrayed his spirit. All the people saw his black deceit. Every day the bucket goes to the well, one day the bottom falls out. (*In agony.*) Aaahh! Eeyaaghooouugh!

She writhes in pain.
As MARCIA *writhes in agony,* SYBIL *leaves her table and slowly approaches* MARCIA's. *She moves only while* MARCIA *wails.*

MARCIA. When they caught him at his business they hounded him out a' his birthplace. For two years he carried on his practice round about Port Antonio. Then it happened all over again just the same. Aaaah!

She writhes, falls and pulls the vase and tablecloth off the table.

SYBIL. Pick it up.

Pause.

MARCIA. Eeyaaghooouugh!

SYBIL. There *is*.

MARCIA. No!

SYBIL. Room. For me. There is.

Pause.

MARCIA. They knocked him about, cut out his tongue. He went home. He died. They buried him like a dog.

SYBIL. Pick – it – up.

MARCIA *picks up the table and resets the vase, flowers and cloth.*
She sits. The pain has gone.

iii.

MARGARET, *white, middle-class, comes on and sits on A2.*

MARGARET. She said an evil spirit is angry with me. She said she could break the spell. She couldn't. Now I'm desperate. Is it a spell that causes damp? All the methods I've found for casting off spells have no effect whatsoever. And I've looked up damp as well. It's not in anything. I've spent hundreds. And builders aren't cheap. As you know.

MARCIA (*deep voice*). Baron Sunday.

MARGARET. Yes. Yes, I heard you, dear. Can you help me or not? You see, in the past I believe there was a West Indian family . . . When we bought it we had the place stripped, of course, top to toe. Even so –

MARCIA. Blood.

MARGARET. Yes?

Baron Sunday: 'My dear, I'm sure hyper-ventilation is a valuable aid but are you quite sure you're all right?'
(Margaret: Tricia Kelly; Sybil: Marjorie Yates; Marcia: Dona Croll)

MARCIA. Of a mongoose.

SYBIL. I don't believe it.

MARGARET. I've tried that. Not exactly with a mongoose. Could that be why?

Pause.
MARCIA *is hyper-ventilating loudly.*

MARCIA. Baron Sunday.

As she speaks, SYBIL *arrives at A3 and sits.*

SYBIL. Damp proofing. Tell her. Don't skimp. Gypsum, sand, proper chemicals. Tell her.

MARGARET. My dear, I'm sure hyper-ventilation *is* a valuable aid but – are you quite sure you're all right?

iv.

MARCIA *is laying table B with cloth, cutlery and plates.*
SYBIL *sits on A1.*

SYBIL. Voodoo. Juju. Tomtom. You want to stay in this basement forever? Voodoo, juju, tomtom – you will.

MARCIA. I'm gonna need that chair.

MARCIA *goes on laying the table.*

SYBIL. Didn't I tell you? Tap the teaspoon three times on the back of your hand before you lay it down. That's how it's done in this country. Go on.

MARCIA. This is my things! I got Jojo an' Big Bonus and all the family comin'. I'm gonna need all the chairs.

SYBIL. Go on!

MARCIA *taps a teaspoon three times on the back of her hand before laying it down.*

MARCIA. I don' want you here.

SYBIL. Good. Now, the knife. The knife must always be pressed against the forehead. It keeps it honed sharp. Try.

Pause.
MARCIA *pulls up the sides of the cloth into a bundle with cutlery and crockery inside. She holds it over her shoulder.*

MARCIA. What's your name?

SYBIL. Today? The princess.

MARCIA. I get on good with Baron Sunday. I don't want no princess.

SYBIL. Put everything back on the table like I told you. Go on.

v.

SYBIL *sitting at A1.*
MARCIA *and* DECIMA *in* DECIMA's *room.*

MARCIA. I think it's time I went back home. I talked to my mother. She agrees. She says this place is workin' on me an' workin' on me. I don't know how she knows the things she knows. She just knows. I am bein' worked on. I don't intend to stay at home forever. But for me to go is good, you think so? My doctor said I'm just not feeling right in myself. She understands me. I got to go back home and find myself. I lost myself. I don't know where.

DECIMA. How's ol' Baron Sunday?

MARCIA. Oh, my head is painin' me.

DECIMA. I got a message for that ol' Baron.

MARCIA. It's painin'. You don' care 'bout that?

DECIMA. Your head? It's bad?

MARCIA. Bad?

DECIMA. I'll go get a aspirin for you.

DECIMA goes out.

SYBIL. The musicologist's booked for half past three. *He* won't be late.

DECIMA comes in with an aspirin and a glass of water. She hands them to MARCIA.

DECIMA. You tell the Baron I found my bracelet. I'm gonna get a refund of all my ten p's?

As DECIMA speaks, MARCIA holds the aspirin in her left fist and makes a circle round it with the glass of water in her right hand. She does this five times.

DECIMA. You feelin' all right, girl?

MARCIA. Some people live here and live here. They never learn nothin'.

vi.

MARCIA *on A1*, SYBIL *on A3*, CURZON, *a white musicologist, on A2.*
MARCIA *is hyper-ventilating but not loudly. She tries to speak. No words come out.*
CURZON *writes as SYBIL speaks.*

SYBIL (*different voice, German accent*). Quaver G, semi-quaver F, quaver E, semi-quaver D –

CURZON. D or D sharp?

SYBIL. D! D natural! Vot you tink I'm writink? Gypsy dances?

MARCIA tries to speak. No words come out.
SYBIL pulls her chair down next to MARCIA's.
MARCIA cries out in agony. No sound is heard.

SYBIL. Demi-quavers E and F, quaver G and G again. Got it?

CURZON. Got it.

SYBIL. Now the second theme.

CURZON turns the page of his notebook, his pencil poised to write.

vii.

SYBIL *on A1*, MARGARET *on A2*, MARCIA *on B3.*

SYBIL (MARCIA*'s voice, West Indian accent*). I been away back home. That's why it took so long to answer your letter. I wanted to go back home. But I found I got no spirit for my ol' home. I got nothin' for it at all. You wan' talk to the spirit?

MARGARET. Baron Sunday? Yes please.

SYBIL. Baron who? No. I left him.

MARGARET. Then – ?

SYBIL. You want to put your money down or not? I got one, believe me. I got one just for you.

14. Possession

DIONYSOS 1 *and* 2 *dance destructively.*
DEREK *is possessed by* PENTHEUS.

PENTHEUS. This is my city. I love it, leave it alone. Kill the god!

15. Dancing

DIONYSOS *passes* DAN *as he enters, then goes out.*

DAN (*to audience*). I don't believe god is necessarily male.

i.

Towards the back, a male and a female PRISON OFFICER *are sitting together at a table.*
Towards the front, a WOMAN *is sitting on a chair wearing a hat.*
DAN, *the vicar, dances to her.*
This dance is precisely the dance that the woman in the chair longs for. Watching it she dies of pleasure.
After a few moments of DAN's *dance, the* PRISON OFFICERS *start to speak.*

FEMALE PRISON OFFICER. All right, a mistake's a mistake. But – this. No, you're kidding me.

MALE PRISON OFFICER. It wasn't our mistake.

FEMALE PRISON OFFICER. You admitted him.

MALE PRISON OFFICER. Her.

FEMALE PRISON OFFICER. Her.

MALE PRISON OFFICER. It was him when we admitted her. I can guarantee that.

FEMALE PRISON OFFICER. Guarantee?

MALE PRISON OFFICER. You want a cup of coffee? Guarantee!

FEMALE PRISON OFFICER. You tell me it's Tuesday, I'm going to write down Easter Sunday, that I guarantee.

MALE PRISON OFFICER. I'm asking, you want coffee?

FEMALE PRISON OFFICER. I don't touch it. Heart.

The MALE PRISON OFFICER *starts making coffee.*

MALE PRISON OFFICER. I didn't put my finger up. If that's what it takes to guarantee, you're right, I can't guarantee.

FEMALE PRISON OFFICER. You said when she came in here she was a he. Have I got it correct?

Dancing: Dan dances precisely the dance that the woman in the chair longs for.
(Dan: Stephen Goff; Victim: Dona Croll)

MALE PRISON OFFICER. What are you trying to say to me? You'll take him –

FEMALE PRISON OFFICER. Her.

MALE PRISON OFFICER. – or you won't take him? Her! The governor's waiting.

FEMALE PRISON OFFICER. He's a convicted multiple killer. He comes into your place
a man. Now they want to transfer him from your place to mine. Pour me that coffee. My
nerves, they can't stand it. Be straight with me, Tommy. What the hell's going on?

The WOMAN *on the chair has died.*
DAN *stops dancing and hauls out the body.*

ii.

A MAN *sits on the chair wearing the hat.*
The MALE PRISON OFFICER *extracts from a large file various pieces of paper. He reads
from one. The difficulty he has with reading produces a flat, matter-of-fact tone. Often he
stumbles. When he loses interest in a passage, he skips.*

MALE PRISON OFFICER. 'My plan was that they should all be good deaths. Clean,
effortless, without tension or pain. To die of pleasure, like a young boy slipping through
the mirror of a mountain stream. These are the deaths the earth needs to grow strong. We
have asked too much of the earth. We take from her everything that is good. What do we
give back? Lives that end in hatred and agony. Our rejected, our despised. So why should
the rain . . .'

DAN *speaks to the* MAN *on the chair.*

DAN. Hi. I'm Dan. Don't think I'm pushy. Uh, you know how it is. You see someone
attractive at the other end of the bar. But you're shy. I'm not shy. What would you like?
What would you really like? I can get you anything you like.

The MAN *on the chair looks at* DAN *intrigued.*
DAN *dances to him.*

MALE PRISON OFFICER. '. . . From the age of seventeen I studied theology at the
university of Saint Cecille outside Brussels. One summer I worked in a vineyard near
Antwerp. The grapes were stillborn. The vineyard failed. O cowards! Embrace the earth
willingly! Why don't you? How can she do you harm? Press your throats against
her boulders. Rip them. Why not, if that is what she wants? What has she ever refused
you? . . .'

'. . . They will say I have tried to play god. I have not. God makes and destroys. I make
and destroy nothing. I do man's work. I transform.'

'Fools! You ransack the guts of the earth –'

I can't make out this bit. Call this handwriting? You wouldn't think he'd been educated at
all. You want to hear any more of this?

The MAN *in the chair dies.*
DAN *stops dancing and hauls out the body.*

iii.

A WOMAN *sits on the chair wearing the hat.*
DAN *puts his head in her lap and talks to her.*

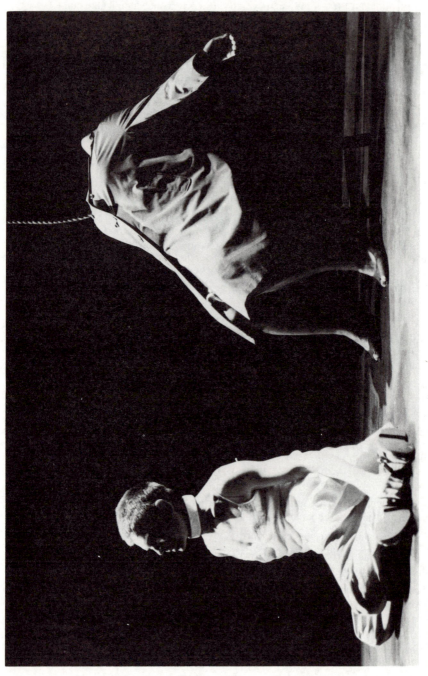

Dancing. The woman in the chair dies of pleasure

DAN. I want to be milked from the udder of a cow. I'd like a pine tree to grow inside me. I want to rest the tips of my fingers on the peaks of two mountains so my muscles tear. I want to burn. And you?

DAN dances briefly to her.
The WOMAN *dies.*
DAN stops dancing and hauls out the body.

iv.

The two PRISON OFFICERS *are sitting in different positions at the table drinking coffee.*
On the chair is the hat.
DAN dances to it.

FEMALE PRISON OFFICER. You must have been killing yourself. Did you know what you were letting me in for? Pass the sugar. I find my girls lying in the corridors, the workshops, the latrines. Dead. Untouched. Beautiful. I know she done it – all of them. Ask me how. Ask me.

MALE PRISON OFFICER. How?

FEMALE PRISON OFFICER. That's what I say – capital punishment. Finish her off – quick smart! But they won't. I have to look after my girls. You know what I done? Ask me.

MALE PRISON OFFICER. What?

FEMALE PRISON OFFICER. What could I do? I let her go.

They go on drinking their coffee.
DAN continues dancing to the chair.
DAN finishes and goes.

16. Possession

DIONYSOS *appears to* DOREEN *and* DEREK.
DOREEN *is possessed by* AGAVE, DEREK *by* PENTHEUS.

PENTHEUS. Mother! Why have the women left the city?

AGAVE. I'm happy. Leave us alone.

PENTHEUS. I'm hungry.

AGAVE *laughs with joy.*

PENTHEUS. I'll fill the woods with blood.

17. Pig

PAUL (*to audience*). That way we make more profit.

i.

PAUL, *a businessman in a suit, is presenting a report to colleagues.*
Meanwhile the PIG *is dancing. The* COLLEAGUES *don't notice the dance.* PAUL'*s attention sometimes goes to it against his will but mainly he is concentrated on what he is doing.*

PAUL. Page 103 refers back pages 78 and 22. Tables E and F correlate in major areas though not as regards beef surplus requirements for Benelux countries. Reliable figures are still unavailable. The improvement in UK exports remains steady, as you will see in my conclusions, but – and here there is, I agree, room for discussion – no substantial acceleration will occur until tariffs are genuinely equalised between all trading partners. The details of what is required as a matter of urgency are found in Appendix E paragraphs 42 to 67.
I hope you will find my conclusions realistic and acceptable. If benefits are to be widespread, duties must remain low. That is uncontested. But the attractions of higher priced European pork, beef and lamb for our own internal domestic markets must be increased if established commercial avenues are to be kept open, standards maintained and profitability stabilised. Turin may wish to go her own way. She will find she cannot. The reasons I hope are now clear.

ii.

PAUL *and* COLLEAGUE.
PIG *continues dancing through beginning of this but comes to an end and goes off without* PAUL *noticing.*

COLLEAGUE. Brilliant report.

PAUL. Thank you.

COLLEAGUE. I only had a slight problem with section 6.2.

PAUL. We must talk about it.

COLLEAGUE. And the column of figures at the top of page 52, I'm probably confused but they don't seem to correlate with the March-April statistics for Belgium.

PAUL. That's an interesting point.

COLLEAGUE. And one other thing, when it says twenty-four million here, I can't for the life of me see where it comes from.

PAUL. Tomorrow morning?

COLLEAGUE. Certainly, no hurry, say ten o'clock? You look as if you could use a drink.

PAUL. Thank you, no. I have an appointment.

   PAUL *turns towards the* PIG *but he's gone.*

iii.

PAUL *drinking with a* FRIEND.

PAUL. I've never noticed pigs before.

FRIEND. If you drive past a pig farm you notice the smell.

PAUL. But really they are very clean animals.

FRIEND. They lie about in the mud. Filthy pig.

PAUL. It depends how they're kept. Sometimes they lie in mud to get cool. That must be nice.

FRIEND. Nice?

PAUL. Like a swimming pool or a sauna. All together in a jacuzzi.

FRIEND. In mud?

PAUL. Women put mud packs on their faces. Children like it. There's a tribe in New Guinea who put mud – No? No. Anyway they don't go in the mud very much. They are very clean. They don't smell if they're kept properly.

FRIEND. So you're off to Italy next week?

PAUL. And anyway it's not such a bad smell. No, no I can't get away at the moment.

FRIEND. I thought you'd booked a villa.

PAUL. Yes, but no, I can't, unfortunately, no. I can't leave just now.

FRIEND. I'm off to Spain myself.

PAUL. They are also very intelligent, did you know that?

FRIEND. Sorry?

PAUL. Pigs. Are very intelligent. Like a dog. More than a dog.

FRIEND. Really?

PAUL. Yes, you can train them. I was reading about it. Somebody lived with a pig in his house. You can housetrain a pig. It comes when you call its name.

FRIEND. Applesauce!

PAUL. It could sleep on the end of your bed.

FRIEND. Bring your slippers and lick your face.

PAUL. They are quite affectionate. If they know you. And in Moscow they have them in the circus, they do the trapeze. They are not fat.

FRIEND. Of course they're fat. Fat pig./ Pig ignorant.

PAUL. They are not fat. They are fattened. They are made fat. We could be fat.

FRIEND. Some of us are.

PAUL. There you are.

FRIEND. But pigs are fat.

PAUL. They are not fat. If a pig has exercise it isn't fat. It's solid but it's strong. Pigs are very strong. They are quite dangerous.

FRIEND. Wild boar of course. Kill them with a pack of dogs.

PAUL. They have tusks. They can kill the dogs. But even your domestic pig can be dangerous. They have a huge bite. Have you looked at their mouths? They've eaten babies. They can bite through metal. And at the same time they are so gentle. You can stroke their ears. Their ears have blue veins.

FRIEND. Silk purse out of a sow's ear.

PAUL. I prefer the ear. Really.

FRIEND. Since when were you a pig fan then?

PAUL. I went to a pig farm last week.

FRIEND. I've been to a pig farm.

PAUL. Yes, I've often done it, of course. But I'd never noticed a pig before. There was one pig I noticed. Once I started looking at him . . . I tried to look at them all again as so many hundred pigs, so many kilos.

FRIEND. As exports.

PAUL. Yes, as percentages. But I came back to this pig.

FRIEND. I'm fond of animals myself. Everyone is, basically. It's recreation, a pet.

PAUL. Yes.

iv.

PAUL *dances with the* PIG, *tenderly.*

v.

PAUL *and his wife,* JUNE. *She is eating fruit.*

JUNE. So can we go on the 23rd?

PAUL. I don't know.

JUNE. We have to make plans.

PAUL. Make the booking. You can always go without me.

JUNE. I just might go without you.

PAUL. No of course. I'll come. Make the booking. That's fine.

JUNE. How was your day.

PAUL. Good, a good day. Long meeting.

JUNE. Did you go to your pig farm again?

PAUL. Yes, I think so. Yes, I did, of course.

JUNE. You really like that pig, don't you?

PAUL. It's amusing.

JUNE. Do you want to get a piglet as a pet? We could try it. People keep snakes and eagles, I could probably cope with a pig.

PAUL. No, no, I don't want to. Thank you.

JUNE. If you'd like it.

PAUL. It's not any pig.

JUNE. How do you mean?

PAUL. It's that pig. I like that pig.

JUNE. Why?

PAUL. It's just – Can I explain this to you, please. You look at him, you just – You don't

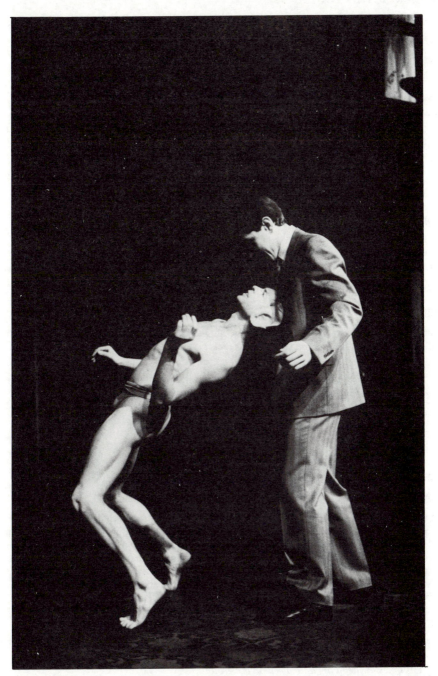

PIG: Paul dances with the Pig, tenderly. (Paul: Philippe Giraudeau; Pig: Stephen Goff)

want to do anything else. His shape is cut in the air. You feel completely – there is nothing else to be said. There he is – and . . .

JUNE. Are you in love with this pig?

PAUL. Of course not.

JUNE. You sound like it.

PAUL. I'm fond of it, yes, people get fond of animals don't they, this is usual, people have animals they are fond of. People leave money to cats. They have tombstones for dogs. I am interested in the pig, that's all.

JUNE. So you don't mind leaving him to go on holiday?

PAUL. That's nothing to do with the pig. I'm very busy.

JUNE. So we can go away and leave the pig?

PAUL. Of course.

JUNE. I'm only teasing. You're so funny.

vi.

PAUL *and the* PIG *dance, dangerously.*

viii.

A COLLEAGUE *is reading a report to* PAUL *and another* COLLEAGUE. *Meanwhile the* PIG *is wrapped in clingfilm. It is now dead meat.*

COLLEAGUE. In the second column we have the agricultural levies for financial year 1986. Belgium 186 billion, Denmark 7 billion, Italy 313 billion, 300 thousand, Germany 187½ billion, Germany 26 billion . . .

She stops and looks at PAUL *who is smiling to himself.*

Germany 187½ billion, Greece 26 billion, France 96 billion, Spain –.

PAUL. I'm sorry. I'm just so happy.

viii.

PAUL *and* FRIEND.

PAUL. I telephoned. They said they were going to be slaughtered that afternoon. I said I would buy my pig. They said which pig, I didn't know, I said I would come at once. I got in the car. It's a two-hour drive. I go there sometimes at night just to stand in the yard, it's an hour and a half at night but during the day it's two hours. There was a traffic jam on the motorway, there'd been an accident. I had to be there by twelve, I arrived at twelve-thirty, they'd sent them off to the abattoir. I drove to the abattoir. It's hard to drive when you're crying.

ix.

PAUL *tears up the documents and scatters them. He rips his jacket off and knocks over the furniture.*
PAUL *takes the dead pig and lays it on the ground.*
He takes off the clingfilm.
The PIG *comes out alive.*
PAUL *and the* PIG *dance, tenderly, dangerously, joyfully.*

Extreme Happiness. (Marjorie Yates, Stephen Goff, Vivienne Rochester, Tricia Kelly, Dona Croll, Philippe Giraudeau)

Extreme Happiness. (Tricia Kelly, Dona Croll, Philippe Giraudeau,
Vivienne Rochester)

18. Extreme happiness

Whole COMPANY *as their main characters.*
This dance consists of memories of moments of extreme happiness.
After a while all the members of the COMPANY *find themselves in a waterfall. They dash in and out, they stand letting the stream pour down on their backs – a moment of severe physical pleasure.*
In the midst of this, the four WOMEN *become possessed by* AGAVE *and the spirits of three* BACCHANTS.
DOREEN *is possessed by* AGAVE:

AGAVE. Why are my feet cut and blistered? I've been running all night.

   MARCIA *is possessed by a* BACCHANT:

BACCHANT 1. Honey in my hair!

   YVONNE *is possessed by a* BACCHANT:

BACCHANT 2 (*of the waterfall*). It's wine!

   LENA *is possessed by a* BACCHANT:

BACCHANT 3. Salt and sweet. I can feel its heart throb!

   Interval

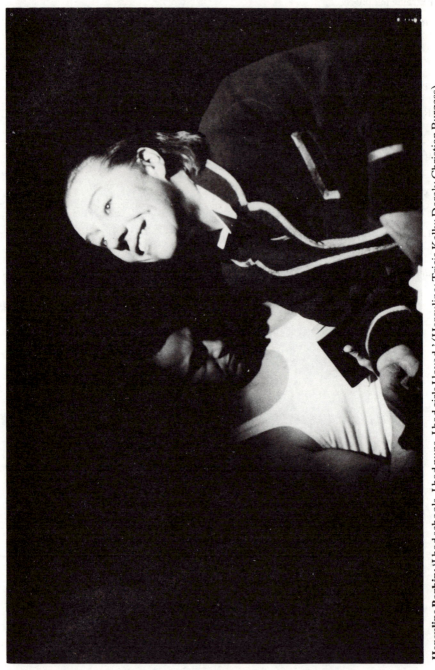

Herculine Barbin: 'I had schools, I had nuns, I had girls I loved.' (Herculine: Tricia Kelly; Derek: Christian Burgess)

ACT TWO

19. Herculine Barbin

DIONYSOS *appears to* DEREK *and stays throughout the scene.*
DEREK *is exercising with weights.*

DEREK (*to audience*). He thought he wasn't a man without a job.

> HERCULINE BARBIN *enters.*
> *She is played by a woman but dressed in the clothes of a Frenchman of the nineteenth century.*
> *While she talks she gives* DEREK *objects from her past which she takes from a small suitcase.*

HERCULINE. Couldn't I have stayed with her? No one was stopping us, I was the one who – and afterwards it would even have been legal, she still loved me then, I must have lost my mind for a while. Blame her mother, (*gives a book*) refusing to notice, have some apricot tart children, my daughter's dearest friend, a daughter to me, goodbye dear daughter, goodbye. Why didn't I keep hold of those hands? Blame yourself, kill yourself.

Abel Barbin, suicide, they'll find the body of a man in the morning, no one will doubt it. Was I really Herculine Barbin, playing by the sea, starting school at the convent, nobody doubted I was a girl. Hermaphrodite, the doctors were fascinated, how to define this body, does it fascinate you, it doesn't fascinate me, let it die.

Where are the girls I loved? They go on not appearing every minute, sometimes it eases, often what I am saying often it eases completely, oh it's not like it was I can have a good – an eyelid, the fall of a skirt, a startling tenderness at the next table, and gone again, all my loves and Sara, Sara and the air, you don't notice your breath till something stops it.

I had schools, I had nuns, I had girls I loved even only a little, no, wholly each time but more and – Lea, so old, seventeen, I was twelve, leaning on me in the garden, I took her a pretty crucifix at night, (*gives a rose*) Mother Superior made me cry. Was I really a lady's maid, undressing Clothilde, combing her hair, it was my job, she got married, no one worried about my body, my periods would come in time.

Hair on my face and arms, cut it with scissors, worse; I kissed Thecla on the mouth. Clever with books, clumsy at sewing, lightning struck, leapt out of bed naked into the nun's arms, feelings of shame I didn't understand. Sinking in sand (*gives scissors and a comb*) up to our knees, laughing, three in a bed, they took off their skirts and tucked up their petticoats, the water splashed high, I was the only one who stayed on the beach.

Where it led, to Sara, I wouldn't let her get dressed without me, stroked her hair, kissed her neck, she put my hand aside and gazed in amazement. Mysterious pains, (*gives crucifix*) she took me into her bed to comfort me, god, Sara was mine, romantic words, Sara is mine, nobody knew, this lasted a long time, the children watched, her hair fell down. In the middle of class she would smile at me.

The pains, the doctor, I screamed, he could hardly speak, but still he didn't stop us, her mother didn't, nobody would admit, I did it myself in the vacation, did I have to? The bishop, very kind, his own doctor, yes I should be declared a man, (*gives the lace shawl.*) the documents, Sara's grief, have some tart dear daughter, couldn't I have asked to marry her, goodbye dear daughter, how to hold my body as a man.

Soon less jeering, job in the railroad, long time with no job, sit in the cafés and see who loves who, at least I'm not a man like the men I see. (*gives the petticoat*). Maybe waiter's assistant on ship to America, what to do, everyone thought it must be something good to take me so far away.

Into the unknown, like now, breathing in fumes, soon dead, how to get back, all the girls' bodies, Sara's body, my girl's body, all lost, couldn't you have stayed?

DEREK *holds all the objects and has dressed himself in the shawl and petticoat.*
He sits in the chair and becomes HERCULINE.
She stands beside him and takes the objects from him and packs them into her suitcase.

DEREK. Couldn't I have stayed with her? No one was stopping us, I was the one who – and afterwards it would even have been legal, she still loved me then, I must have lost my mind for a while. Blame her mother, refusing to notice, have some apricot tart children, my daughter's dearest friend, a daughter to me, goodbye dear daughter, goodbye. Why didn't I keep hold of those hands? Blame yourself, kill yourself.

Abel Barbin, suicide, they'll find the body of a man in the morning, no one will doubt it. Was I really Herculine Barbin, playing by the sea, starting school at the convent, nobody doubted I was a girl. Hermaphrodite, the doctors were fascinated, how to define this body, does it fascinate you, it doesn't fascinate me, let it die.

HERCULINE. What's the matter? Be happy. You know I love you.

DEREK. Where are the girls I loved? They go on not appearing every minute, sometimes it eases, often what am I saying often it eases completely, oh it's not like it was I can have a good – an eyelid,/ the fall of a

HERCULINE. Lea, I love you.

DEREK. skirt, a startling tenderness at the next table, and gone again, (*takes away the rose*) all my loves and Sara, Sara and the air, you don't notice your breath till something stops it.

I had schools, I had nuns, I had girls I loved even only a little, no, wholly each time but more and – Lea, so old, seventeen, I was twelve, leaning on me in the garden, I took her a pretty crucifix at night, Mother Superior made me cry. Was I really a lady's maid, undressing Clothilde, combing her hair, it was my job, she got married, no one worried about my body, my periods would come in time.

HERCULINE. May you be happy later, poor child.

DEREK. Hair on my face and arms, cut it with scissors, worse;/ (*takes the book*)

HERCULINE. I'm sorry to hurt you, once more, nearly over.

DEREK. I kissed Thecla on the mouth. Clever with books, clumsy at sewing, lightning struck, leapt out of bed naked into the nun's arms, feelings of shame I didn't understand. Sinking in sand up to our knees,/ (*takes the scissors and comb*)

HERCULINE. Modesty, morality and the respect you owe a religious house.

DEREK. laughing, three in a bed, they took off their skirts and tucked up their petticoats, the water splashed high, I was the only one who stayed on the beach.

Where it led, to Sara,/

HERCULINE. Herculine! come in the water.

DEREK. I wouldn't let her get dressed without me, stroked her hair, kissed her neck, she put my hand aside and gazed in amazement. Mysterious pains, she took me into her bed to comfort me, god, Sara was mine, romantic words, Sara is mine, (*takes the crucifix*) nobody knew, this lasted a long time, the children watched, her hair fell down. In the middle of class she would smile at me.

Herculine Barbin: Herculine turns back and kisses Derek on the neck.

HERCULINE. I've made you an apricot tart.

DEREK. The pains, the doctor, I screamed, he could hardly speak, but still he didn't stop us, her mother didn't, nobody would admit, I did it myself in the vacation, did I have to? The bishop, very kind, his own doctor, yes I should be declared a man, the documents, Sara's grief, have some tart dear daughter, couldn't I have asked to marry her, goodbye dear daughter,/ (*takes the lace shawl*)

HERCULINE. Goodbye, dear daughter.

DEREK. how to hold my body as a man.
     Soon less jeering, job in the railroad, long time with no job, sit in the cafés and see who loves who, at least I'm not a man like the men I see. Maybe waiter's assistant on ship to America, what to do, everyone thought it must be something good to take me so far away.
     Into the unknown, like now, breathing in fumes, soon dead, how to get back, all the girls' bodies, (*takes the petticoat*) Sara's body, my girl's body, all lost,

HERCULINE *starts to go.*

DEREK. couldn't you have stayed?

HERCULINE *turns back and kisses him on the neck.*

20. Possession

DIONYSOS *approaches* DEREK.
DEREK *is possessed by* PENTHEUS:

PENTHEUS. Send the soldiers to fetch the women. I want to kill them. I want to see them. I'll go to the mountain.

21. Gold Shoes

YVONNE's *room.*
DIONYSOS *passes through* YVONNE's *room and goes out.*

YVONNE (*to audience*). What is it makes you so angry?

In another room YVONNE's MOTHER *sits crocheting.*
YVONNE, *a woman in her late twenties, comes in wearing a white housecoat. She sits on the bed, leans over letting her head down between her knees. She sits up, breathes out. Her manner is listless, distracted.*

YVONNE. A – apple. B? Butterfly. C? C – dammit.

She leans back looks around the room.

C, C – what can I see?

She is still.
In the distance – a scrap of music plays three or four bars and stops.

Ma? Ma, are you there?
     A – advocaat. B? Brandy? C? Cognac. D? D, D – Sweet Jesus, get it out of your . . . mind! D, D – what can I – ? Ma! Ma, I'm not going out, ma. You hear me? I swear to you. I am no more going out of this house –. Drambuie! Got it. Right, that's it. Now E!

She is in pain.

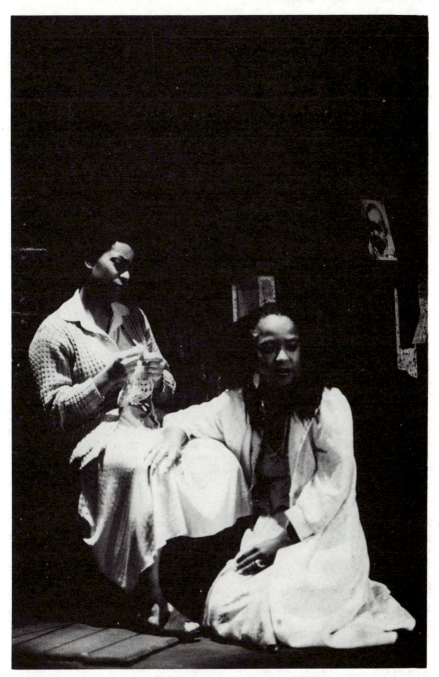

Gold Shoes: 'I'll go to the meeting but I won't go tonight.' (Yvonne: Vivienne Rochester; Mother: Dona Croll)

56   A MOUTHFUL OF BIRDS

Oh! I can't bear – can't bear . . .

She gets up, takes off her housecoat. She wears a light cotton dress underneath. She stands with her housecoat over her arm.

Um – ladies and gentlemen – no. Friends, my name is Yvonne, I – am –. I am an –.

She stops, thinks, lies on the bed.

Ma?

She starts to rise from the bed. As she lifts herself away from the bed the music returns, the same few bars – deafeningly loud.
During the music enter two WOMEN (WOMAN A and WOMAN B). They sit drinking and leafing through fashion magazines. Both WOMEN are dressed in smart evening clothes. WOMAN A wears a red dress, WOMAN B wears turquoise. Both wear gold shoes.
When the music ends, YVONNE goes out.
She comes in wearing her white housecoat. As before she sits on the bed, leans over letting her head down between her knees. She sits up, breathes out. Her manner is listless, distracted.

YVONNE. A – apple. B? Butterfly. C? Caramel. D? Doughnut. E? Envelope.

She leans back, looks around the room.

Wilson – you taught me something bad with your alcohol alphabet. I'll wipe my brain clean. F? Frascati. Damn.

She sits up.

I am not! I am not!

She goes over to her mother.

You really got nothing hidden in this whole house? I don't believe it.
    I'm not going out. Tonight I've got to – . So don't ask me to go out for, buy you – whatever. I can't do that now. The roads at this time of the evening? It's not that. That's not it. That's over. I don't feel like that about roads, roads and cars, cars and drivers anymore. To cross roads at night . . . Stand on the pavement, the cars are coming for me, trying to . . . I know they're not trying to crush me . . . You want something, ask Wilson. (*Calls.*) Wilson!

MOTHER. He's gone out.

YVONNE. I'll go to the meeting but I won't go tonight. I can't bear to sit there – ladies . . . my name, Yvonne . . . alcoholic. I'm not an alcoholic. Anyway, tonight I've got to paint the window frame.

She goes back to her bed.

F. Done it. G? Gloss paint.

She gets up, takes off her housecoat, finds a pot of paint and a paint brush. She goes out of the room and reappears with a pair of paint-bespattered dungarees. She kicks off her shoes, slips off her dress. She is wearing a slip underneath. She opens a cupboard. Out falls a pair of gold shoes.
The music returns.
WOMAN A greets WOMAN B with a bright cheery wave.

WOMAN A. Good time?

WOMAN B. Very pleasant.

They go on drinking.
YVONNE picks up the gold shoes and looks at them.
She pulls on the dungarees.
She puts on the gold shoes.
The dungarees fall to the ground and she is dressed exactly like WOMAN A.
The volume of the music rises.
YVONNE dances. She ends up on the bed in despair.
The music fades.
MOTHER waves at the TWO WOMEN.

MOTHER. You should see our Yvonne. What a beauty. What a peach.

The music stops.

You should see our Yvonne. What a pity. Life's a bitch. (*To* YVONNE.) You said you weren't going out.

YVONNE. No.

MOTHER. So why you dressed up for a party? Yvonne? Someone's having a party? You going out, yes or no? You losing control of yourself again? Don't look to me for help. You've worn me out, out, out. I'm finished with your crying, your howling. You want to go out with your smart friends, go out. You got a thought in your head to cut me? Yvonne? I'm not one of your patients for you to stick needles in. You going to cut me again? I'm cut to pieces. Your father cut me there. Doctor – there. That crazy boy at the church cut me here. You cut me there, there, there.

She shows the places.

YVONNE. I –

YVONNE rushes out and comes in immediately wearing the white housecoat.

A – apple. B? Butterfly. C? C –dammit. C, C – what can I see? (*In anguish.*) I never cut you!

MOTHER. Then what's this. And what's this? I don't give you what you're asking, you cut me. You're cutting me up bit by bit like a pig – you know that? Go in that room. Do as you told me. Paint the window frame. Yvonne? You never lied to me. Tell me what it is.

YVONNE. Just one.

MOTHER exhales deeply.
She produces a bottle of gin and puts it on the table.

YVONNE. Oh yes. G for gin.

She drinks.
She takes off the housecoat. YVONNE's *dress is now yellow.* WOMAN A *and* WOMAN B *come into* YVONNE's *room and sit on the bed. She fills their glasses and her own. They all drink.*
The music returns.
YVONNE and the two WOMEN *dance. After a moment,* YVONNE *retches and pulls away from them. The* WOMEN *offer her another drink. She rushes to her bed and kicks off her shoes.*
The music stops.
The TWO WOMEN *return to their places and go on drinking.*

YVONNE. A – apple. B – butterfly. C – caramel. D – doughnut. E – envelope. F? Fire. G?

She pulls her dungarees over her clothes, picks up the paint and brush and starts painting the window frame.
After a moment, she puts down the brush and picks up the gold shoes. She examines them closely, then puts them on.

YVONNE. G for gold shoes.

She goes on painting the window frame.

22. The dressing of Pentheus

In this dance, DEREK *is possessed by* PENTHEUS *and is dressed as a woman by* DIONYSOS 1 *and* DIONYSOS 2.
At first PENTHEUS *attacks* DIONYSOS 1 *and* 2. *They elude him as though it were a game and transform his aggression into acceptance. They dress him in their own clothes so that he is dressed as a woman.*

PENTHEUS. Do I look like my mother?

23. Hot Summer

DIONYSOS *passes* DOREEN *as she enters. He goes out.*

DOREEN (*to the audience*). All I wanted was peace and quiet.

Each in a different room:
MRS BLAIR *is listening to the radio quietly in the room above* DOREEN.
LIL *is reading a newspaper.*
TONY *is chopping vegetables.*
EVANS *is drinking heavily.*
SUSY *is massaging* DOREEN's *neck and shoulders while* DOREEN *talks.*

I don't know which bit of me it's in. My head aches but if you ask me where it's not so much my head, it's more my neck. Or behind my eyes, there's something behind – My shoulders are a mass of knots, anywhere you touch on my shoulders is where the trouble is. Here, there's a spot here, I can't quite – My whole spine if you went down it. There's a pain in my stomach I get if I don't eat and another I get after I've eaten, and another, it's not in the stomach – I don't know where all your tubes are but there's definitely something. And the pain in my shoulders and hips goes right down, my elbows are stiff, my knees seize up, my fingers crack, my toes throb – so from head to foot. Anywhere you touched me would hurt. And that's not even the worst. It's not so much as if I'm going to vomit but every bit of me is nauseated, my left foot wants to vomit, my blood – I'm completely full of this awful sickness.

SUSY *finishes the massage. She kisses the top of* DOREEN's *head and goes to the room she shares with* LIL. LIL *starts quietly reading from the paper. Soon what she is reading is lost beneath the sound of the radios.*
TONY *and* EVANS *continue as before.*

LIL. 'An unemployed Liverpool man was found guilty yesterday of the murder of his wife and two children aged 9 and 4. Michael Burns, 38, told police, "God asked me to send them to him." A neighbour summoned by Burns found the bodies in a bedroom and bathroom. They had been stabbed repeatedly. Burns was described in court as "a quiet

Dressing of Pentheus: Pentheus attacks Dionysos 1 and 2. They elude him. (Pentheus: Christian Burgess; Dionysos 1: Philippe Giraudeau; Dionysos 2: Stephen Goff)

Dressing of Pentheus: Dionysos 1 and 2 dress Pentheus as a woman.

friendly man who never raised his voice".

'A Turkish villager left prison to find his former girlfriend had married another man. He had been imprisoned for abducting the girl and returned to his village to discover she had married. He shot or knifed to death nine people he met as he searched for her.

'The Victoria line was out of action for two hours last night after a woman, 35, grabbed a stranger and pushed him in front of an approaching train. The victim, a man of 40, died instantly.

'A Manchester woman, 22, who said she feared demons would possess her baby daughter was found not guilty of the child's murder by reason of insanity. The two-month-old girl dressed in pink was found buried in a park with her mouth full of leaves.

'An eighteen-year-old typist pleaded guilty to murdering her flatmate by stabbing her with a carving knife while she slept. She told police, "I just got the knife and went and did it. It seemed important at the time. I didn't have anything against her."

'Police in Los Angeles are looking for a strangler who has raped and killed twelve women in recent months. Their naked bodies have been found on hillsides and in rivers. Their ages range from 13 to 51. Women have been advised not to go out alone after dark and to close all ground floor doors and windows.

'Three youths are being held in Adelaide without bail on charges of having stabbed a man fifty times, poured turpentine into his wounds and cut him to pieces with a butcher's knife. The body of the victim, 42, was found in a black rubbish bag in a neighbour's back yard.

'A fifteen-year-old girl was admitted to hospital yesterday with third degree burns to her face after pouring petrol on her hair and setting light to it.

'Housewife Cindy Johnson, 36, of Little Rock Arkansaw yesterday shot and killed her husband and two of her three children and then killed herself. She used a rifle the family kept to protect themselves from intruders. One of her daughters, Ellen, 17, escaped by jumping from a bedroom window. The youngest child, Luke, 6, was playing outside when his mother called him in and shot him in the kitchen.'

Soon after LIL *has started reading,* DOREEN *turns her radio on.*
MRS BLAIR *turns her radio up.*
DOREEN *turns her radio up.*
MRS BLAIR *turns her radio up and thumps.*
DOREEN *turns her radio up, thumps and shouts.*
MRS BLAIR *turns her radio up, thumps, shouts, and bangs saucepans.*
DOREEN *turns her radio up, thumps, shouts, bangs saucepans and knocks a chair over.*
MRS BLAIR *turns her radio up, thumps, shouts, bangs saucepans and knocks a chair over and smashes crockery.*
DOREEN *turns her radio up, thumps, shouts, bangs saucepans and knocks a chair over, smashes crockery and shakes out a roll of carpet.*
Both radios are now at full volume, both playing different things. It is impossible to hear anything, but LIL *keeps reading aloud.*
MRS BLAIR *continues thumping and shouting.*
DOREEN *rolls up the carpet and unrolls it again.*

Suddenly both rush out of their rooms shouting. They meet. DOREEN *slashes* MRS BLAIR *in the face with a knife.* MRS BLAIR *stands there with blood coming out of her face.* DOREEN *pulls her down onto the floor and rolls her up in the carpet.* DOREEN *pulls the end of the carpet so* MRS BLAIR *is rolled out.* DOREEN *turns off the radio, both radios go off.*

Silence except that LIL *is still reading from the newspaper. Everyone else is still doing what they were doing.*

Hot Summer: Doreen and Mrs Blair banging saucepans. (Doreen: Marjorie Yates; Mrs Blair: Dona Croll; Evans: Philippe Giraudeau; Tony: Stephen Goff)

While LIL *is still reading* MRS BLAIR *goes back to her room and turns the radio on quietly.*
Once the radio is on, LIL *stops reading aloud and* SUSY *goes back to* DOREEN'*s room.* SUSY *now keeps some distance from* DOREEN.

SUSY. We'll go on a coach from Victoria. It only takes an hour. We'll get back in the evening about eight.

DOREEN. I've been up since five.

SUSY. Won't you come though? We can get a boat and go on the river. It won't be so hot.

DOREEN. I don't need sleep anymore. I don't need food.

SUSY. And your back's better.

DOREEN. What's wrong with my back?

SUSY. Nothing, that's good.

DOREEN. There's nothing at all wrong with my back or any other part of me. Do you know that?

SUSY. Yes.

DOREEN. Good.

SUSY. So would you like to come for a day out? It's cool on the river. It's one thing always makes me happy, being in a boat and putting your hand in the water. It makes you feel better.

DOREEN. I don't need a boat. I don't need water. I don't need you coming in here trying to make me better. What? What's better? What?

SUSY. I thought you might like it.

DOREEN. You better get out of the room.

SUSY *goes back to the room she shares with* LIL. MRS BLAIR *still listens to the radio and* EVANS *still drinks.*
TONY *comes to* DOREEN'*s room.*

TONY. Hi, we've seen each other in the hall, my name's Tony. I'm sorry to bother you but I wonder if you could let me have a teabag? I forgot I was out of tea when I went –

DOREEN. You come in a room where I'm perfectly peaceful. How do I know what you are? Teabag? You could be going to put a sack over my head. You could have a knife but I have a knife so think again. /My sister lives with a man who

TONY. Look I only –

DOREEN. poured boiling water over her and she thinks it's her fault.

TONY. Lady, I don't need this.

DOREEN. Anyone can do it. There's nothing can't be used as a weapon. Chair. String. A cup of hot tea.

TONY. You are a crazy, you know that? Suck my cock.
It's a hot night. Now. Let's just –

TONY *goes.*

DOREEN. Tear you up.

Hot Summer: 'I've a friend who swallowed glass.' (Doreen: Marjorie Yates; Susy: Vivienne Rochester)

TONY *goes back to his room. He starts to eat what he prepared.*
DOREEN *bites her arm.*
SUSY *comes back to* DOREEN'*s room. She still keeps her distance but less far than before.*

DOREEN. Once you start fighting you don't stop. There's two ways you end up. One's with six warders on top of you. They drag you so your head bangs on each step. You keep fighting till they stick a needle in and you're glad to be gone out of it. The other way you end up is by yourself. I've done weeks on end. All you've got left is your own piss and shit. A lot of women cut themselves. I've a friend who swallowed glass. I don't want to.

Silence.
SUSY *starts massaging* DOREEN'*s feet.*
LIL *comes to* DOREEN'*s room but keeps her distance.*

SUSY. There are people who can stare at walls and bring them down.

DOREEN. What have you been taking?

SUSY. I think I made a cup fall off the table.

DOREEN. By what?

SUSY. By looking at it. We could try and blow that light.

DOREEN. You're not strong enough. You're a butterfly.

SUSY. I'm getting stronger. Will we try?

DOREEN. Have we really got nothing better to do than this?

The three of them try to blow the light bulb of a lamp by concentrating on it. Silence for some time. Nothing happens.

DOREEN. I'm just going red in the face.

SUSY. One of these days.

TONY *comes into the room.*

TONY. Hi. I was just wondering if any of you guys have got some salad cream –

DOREEN. No.

DOREEN'*s 'No' is quiet but it bounches* TONY *off the walls.*

SUSY. You can do it.

DOREEN. Yes.

She puts out her hand and the lamp comes through the air into it.
DOREEN, SUSY *and* LIL *keep repeating yes and laughing. Objects keep flying across the room.*

24. The Death of Pentheus

DEREK, *still dressed as he was by* DIONYSOS, *is possessed by* PENTHEUS:

PENTHEUS. Kill the god! Kill the god! Kill the god!

PENTHEUS *is brought by* DIONYSOS *into a dance of the whole company in which moments of Extreme Happiness and of violence from earlier parts of the play are repeated.*

Death of Pentheus: Agave leaps on Pentheus. Dionysos 1 and 2 watch.
(Agave: Marjorie Yates; Pentheus: Christian Burgess; Bacchant: Tricia Kelly;
Dionysos 1: Philippe Giraudeau; Dionysos 2: Stephen Goff)

Death of Pentheus: The women attack Pentheus.

Death of Pentheus: The women tear up Pentheus

Apart from DEREK, *all the other actors are dressed in the clothes of their main characters.* PENTHEUS *is torn to pieces by* DOREEN *who is possessed by* AGAVE *and the other* WOMEN *who are possessed by* BACCHANTS.
PAUL/DIONYSOS *and* DAN/DIONYSOS *watch.*
When PENTHEUS *is dead,* AGAVE *and the* BACCHANTS *become quiet and realise what they have done.*

AGAVE. I broke open his ribs. I tore off his head.

She gathers his limbs together.
LENA, YVONNE *and* MARCIA *get up and start to go.*

AGAVE. Where are you going?

LENA. Home.

MARCIA. I'm late for work.

YVONNE. I have to look after someone.

AGAVE. There's nothing for me there. There never was. I'm staying here.

The WOMEN *turn back and stay.*

PART THREE

25. Old people

LENA. Every day is a struggle but that's all right. Old people are very tiring. I'm not squeamish, I used to be, couldn't kill a rabbit, I deal with sick and shit every day. I'm not frightened of anything, I walk alone at night, throw him over my shoulder if I have to. Some of the old ladies know me, some of them don't know anyone. You can get fond of them. You tuck them up like babies. Every day is a struggle because I haven't forgotten anything. I remember I enjoyed doing it. It's nice to make someone alive and it's nice to make someone dead. Either way. That power is what I like best in the world. The struggle is every day not to use it.

26. Meat

YVONNE. Many people are surprised to see a woman behind this counter. They look round the shop. Where's the butcher? I smile, show my teeth. I spend all day sawing and hacking. I have a feel for the strengths of a body. All the men know it. They ask me: slit here or slit there? I close my eyes. Feel. Slit there. When I was young I'd dream. I'd wake and forget. Now I sleep, wake, I'm here. Half of kidneys, pound of stewing. Chop chop!

27. Desert

DAN. Can you believe this was all sand? The most beautiful garden I know is an oasis, high walls round it, peaches, nectarines, figs, the gardener makes sweet syrups from violets and roses. These fields don't compare. But if you'd seen it before. I can't tell you what a day it was when I woke up and saw the first green.

28. Sea

MARCIA. My boat is twenty foot long, twelve foot wide, too small to sail far out. Longing can not carry over water so a short way from the land is far enough. Alone I need nothing. What I want I order with my radio. Hearing voices gives me pain but to test my strength sometimes is good. If I go ashore they'll ask my name. I could tell them – oh, what I could tell them. Horror. What for? At sea, at night the air is silent. I listen. I hear nothing. I am full of joy. Of course, the rocks speak. That's quite different. Most days I sleep. My wish is that I'll never wake to see the sky without a star.

29. Drinking

PAUL. When you stop being in love the day is very empty. It's not just the one you loved who isn't exciting any more, nothing is exciting. Nothing is even bearable. So it wasn't till then that I left my wife and my job. I can't stand small pleasures. If there's nothing there's room for something to come. Sometimes on my third scotch I'd wonder if now . . . so I continued with the scotch. Days are quite long when you sit in the street but it's important not to do anything. It may not be love next time. You can't tell what it's going to be. You're lucky if once in your life. So I stay ready.

30. Body

DEREK. My breasts aren't big but I like them. My waist isn't small but it makes me smile. My shoulders are still strong. And my new shape is the least of it. I smell light and sweet. I come into a room, who has been here? Me. My skin used to wrap me up, now it lets the world in. Was I this all the time? I've almost forgotten the man who possessed this body. I can't remember what he used to be frightened of. I'm in love with a lion-tamer from Kabul. Every day when I wake up, I'm comfortable.

31. Birds

DOREEN. I can find no rest. My head is filled with horrible images. I can't say I actually see them, it's more that I feel them. It seems that my mouth is full of birds which I crunch between my teeth. Their feathers, their blood and broken bones are choking me. I carry on my work as a secretary.

32. DIONYSOS dances.